MAKING YOUR

Marriage Work

MAKING YOUR

Marriage Work

MARY & ANDREW JENSEN

AUGSBURG Publishing House • Minneapolis

MAKING YOUR MARRIAGE WORK

Copyright © 1985 Augsburg Publishing House

Scripture quotations unless otherwise noted are from the Holy Bible: New International Version. Copyright 1978 by the New York International Bible Society. Used by permission of Zondervan Bible Publishers.

Library of Congress Cataloging in Publication Data

Jensen, Mary E.
  MAKING YOUR MARRIAGE WORK.

  1. Marriage.   2. Marriage—Religious aspects.
I. Jensen, Andrew, 1938-   II. Title.
HQ734.J43   1985   306.8'1   85-7528
ISBN 0-8066-2124-9

Manufactured in the U.S.A.   APH 10-4265

1   2   3   4   5   6   7   8   9   0   1   2   3   4   5   6   7   8   9

To the many people
who shared their marriage experiences and insights
with us so this book could "ring true."
It was a privilege
to be trusted with so many personal
and precious memories.

Contents

Foreword   9
About This Book and How to Use It   11

1   When Communication Problems Exist   17
2   When a Couple Seeks Counseling   25
3   When a Couple Copes with Two Careers   31
4   When the Children Leave Home   37
5   When a Couple's Friends Are Being Divorced   43
6   When Difficulties Arise with Parents
    or Parents-in-Law   49
7   When a Couple Retires   55
8   When Addiction Results in Alienation   61
9   When Former Marriages Are a Factor   67
10   When a Couple's Child Dies   73
11   When an Older Parent Lives with a Couple   81
12   When a Couple Copes with Unemployment   87
13   When Childbearing Involves a Choice   93
14   When Violence and Abuse Erupt   99
15   When a Couple Moves to a New Location   105
16   When Unfaithfulness Results in Disease   111
17   When a Couple's Priorities Are Distorted   117
18   When a Couple's Child Is in Trouble   123
19   When a Couple Is Divided over Religion   129
20   When Rights and Respect Are Demanded   135

Research Questionnaire   141

Foreword

These 20 vignettes of marriage, while purportedly fictional, are sharply engaging, totally relevant for our lives today, and written in a style that quickly engages and draws one into the story. *Making Your Marriage Work* is a genuinely helpful vehicle for much-needed ministry.

Lee M. Griffin, M.D.
Consultant for Pastoral Care

▪ About This Book and ▪
How to Use It

Marriage is the most complicated of human relationships. Being a mother, father, son, daughter, brother, or sister involves a family tie that, although sometimes difficult, is very strong. This is a "blood" relationship, and it means commitment. Being a friend involves a similarity of interests and attitudes that, although pleasant, does not signify lifelong commitment, especially if the relationship becomes strained or dull.

Marriage, on the other hand, does not involve a blood relationship or a family tie, nor does it involve the necessity of similar interests, attitudes, or backgrounds. In our culture a wedding usually occurs when a man and a woman are in love. They make a commitment to each other based on that love. A wedding occurs, but the marriage is yet to be forged. Only time, work, and experience will make a marriage out of the union created at the wedding.

This is often a bumpy, even rocky, road to travel together. Think about it: two people have become attracted to each other and have made promises of commitment. Each person has been raised in a particular type of home, has been taught different values, has experienced unique life-styles and family relation-ships. Certain customs have been practiced, certain foods have been enjoyed, certain habits have been cultivated. Life has provided each person with different joys or problems, different educational and work opportunities, different physical powers, capabilities, and potentials. Each person has his or her own set of dreams and expectations, not to mention his or her own one-of-a-kind personality.

When the wedding occurs, most couples are romantically expecting a "happy-ever-after" result. They quickly discover the real world; life settles into a routine, and the romantic cloud begins to dissipate. The two different sets of life expe-riences now come to the fore, and these are compounded with other circumstances from the outside: a new job, a move to a new community, living with or near parents, the arrival of a child, the influence of friends, and a multitude of other pres-sures. As the months and years progress, a couple either blends their varied backgrounds and grows closer through the ac-cumulation of experiences, or the partners gradually separate from each other because they are not able to pull backgrounds and experiences together. These factors become divisive instead of unifying.

Christians believe that Jesus Christ lived, died, and rose again to save people from their sins. Human beings are not able to pull themselves out of the muck and mire of sin. We need our Savior to do that for us. Often, however, Christians don't translate the concept of personal sin to their daily ex-periences or to the world. Our Christian understanding needs to include the recognition that we live in a broken world, that sin has entered every experience and every relationship. It shouldn't surprise us to discover that the marriage relationship has also been broken.

The initial reaction to this kind of message may be despair: "If it's broken and sinful, what's the use? Why should I even try to make things better?" This is compounded when the fact is emphasized that as human beings we are unable to save ourselves. The good news is that Christ has entered into our lives *and* our world. There is no cause for despair when we claim the ultimate promise that Christ is "making all things new" (Rev. 21:5).

That still leaves us with yesterday and today and all the tomorrows that will occur before Christ brings about that brand-new world. In the meantime how do we live our days and how do we cope with our relationships in this broken world? The answer is a paradox, a both/and experience. We depend completely on the Lord Jesus to work his saving grace in our lives, trusting that even in the midst of this broken world his redemptive work takes place. At the same time we work hard, remembering that God has not left us without gifts, using the talents, insights, and tools he has provided to effect and promote newness, love, and peace in our relationships. Tools the Lord has given human beings include training and expertise, medical and scientific discoveries, psychological understandings, money and material possessions, life experiences, and even laughter and good humor. Through it all, Christians will be close to the Lord Jesus through Word, sacrament, and prayer, claiming the gifts of love, hope, forgiveness, and salvation.

Not every marriage will succeed; not every situation will be wonderful. The brokenness of relationships and of the world is a fact that Christians and non-Christians alike must face. Christians are not exempt from problems, nor does our faith include magic words that automatically ensure a good marriage. But Christians have spiritual tools to cope with the world's brokenness. Even when a situation is difficult or a relationship in shreds, these tools of faith and hope can bring love and understanding to bear, along with the confidence that the Lord can use even our most feeble efforts for his glory.

▪ How to Use This Book ▪

The short-story format has been used in this discussion of marriage because the reality, drama, joy, and pathos of peoples' lives can be depicted so vividly in fiction. We tend to identify with a story's characters—reflecting, learning, and gaining perspectives by sharing their experiences for a moment in time.

Jesus used stories to teach important truths about the kingdom of God. His teachings involved people, settings, and incidents that were familiar, that "rang true" to his listeners. Even today Jesus' stories of the good Samaritan and the prodigal son, for instance, are known even by people who are otherwise unfamiliar with the Bible.

Stories that use the familiar to show the way to the new and unfamiliar are comfortable avenues for insight and knowledge. The characters prepare the way by treading the strange ground ahead, by showing the possibilities for change and growth. Such stories linger with us long after the book has been closed.

These 20 stories provide glimpses of married couples in moments of joy, fear, anger, frustration, sorrow, understanding, caring, and love. The glimpses are designed to lead into larger pictures and insights about marriage, our partners, ourselves, and other people. The stories are meant to allow a glimmer of truth and understanding to penetrate into dark, static, and seemingly hopeless situations and relationships. The stories are open-ended, without complete resolution, allowing thought and discussion to occur.

The questions at the end of each story may be used as individual thought-stretchers or for discussion by a couple or in small groups. Counselors may find the questions to be valuable discussion-starters in marriage-counseling sessions or as "homework" assignments.

The short stories and questions are intended to be catalysts for communication. As quickly becomes apparent in the stories, communication in marriage is of paramount importance. Without talking and sharing, two people go their separate ways; with minimal communication, a couple experiences misunderstandings and loneliness; with active communication, a couple constructs and strengthens the marriage, using the varied backgrounds and the shared experiences as building blocks for a strong and vital relationship.

At the end of the book is one of the questionnaires used in the background research for the stories. Couples may find, as did the interviewed people, that the open-ended statements are thought-provoking communication tools.

The ideas and background for the stories came from the authors' own marriage experience of 23 years, from observations and counseling of many other couples, and from interviews and questionnaires done specifically for this book. The stories and their characters are fictional, but the problems, the emotions, the situations, and the dreams are very real.

1

▪ When Communication ▪ Problems Exist

"What is your problem, Jim?" Barbara demanded. "That weekend is more than six weeks away. And it's in August when the teams haven't come on campus yet. Why can't we sign up to go on the couples' retreat?"

"Look, I just don't want to commit myself to being away a whole weekend. Football practice will be starting the next week, and I'll probably need to be around to get it all organized. Besides," Jim said, pushing his chair back from the dinner table, "why in the world do you want to go on a couples' retreat? We don't even belong to the couples' club at church. You always said it was too cute and schmaltzy."

"I know I did, and I still think hayrides and sing-alongs are not for us," Barbara said. "But this is different, Jim. They've got a husband-and-wife team, a psychologist and a marriage counselor, coming all the way from Denver to be the speakers. I think it'll be a worthwhile weekend. And we need all the help we can get."

"And what does *that* mean?" Jim asked with an edge to his voice. "We've been married six years, and we're still together. What kind of help do you think we need?" He stood up, crossed his arms and shifted his weight to one leg, challenging his wife. "Do you think there's something wrong with our marriage?"

Barbara stood up too, and began to clear the dishes from the table. "I just think we can use some help, that's all. The speakers are going to be teaching skills in communication. We sure can benefit from that. We hardly ever talk to each other."

Jim snorted a gruff, humorless laugh. "Face it, Barbara. We have very little to talk about. You're so busy with your fancy job and friends and with your la-di-da concerts and ballets that you don't pay any attention to what I enjoy."

Barbara slammed the dishes on the counter. "And you're so gung ho on football, wrestling, and weight lifting that you don't even *want* to hear about *my* interests. How we ever got together is a mystery to me."

"You were pretty impressed with my football playing when we were in college, you know. You came to all the games, and you knew the plays. But when we were married, you suddenly changed. Then you didn't like football. Wrestling was gross, and weight lifting was boring. You can't have it both ways, Barbara Jean." Jim followed his wife into the kitchen work area and glowered at her.

"Look who's talking," Barbara countered, barely letting him finish his sentence. "You should sharpen your memory, Mr. Football Hero. When we were in college, you took me to concerts and the ballet as well as to lovely restaurants. Then you said you enjoyed it, that it brought beautiful culture and variety into your life. Now you make fun of me for liking those things, and you refuse to share them with me anymore. Why should I go to your stupid football games when you won't share *my* interests?"

Jim and Barbara stood at dueling range, arms crossed, glaring at each other. The anger was thick between them. Then Barbara dropped her arms to her sides and took a deep breath, letting it out in a big sigh.

"We're doing it again, Jim. We're sniping at each other and getting nowhere. I just thought a weekend away learning how to communicate might help us. Aren't you tired of fighting?" Jim still stood with his arms crossed, but he'd dropped his gaze to the floor.

Barbara scraped the dishes, then loaded the dishwasher. Turning off the lights, she walked slowly into the living room. Jim was sitting in the big, comfortable rocker, moving it back and forth.

"I'm sorry I said those things, Jim," Barbara murmured, patting him on the shoulder as she walked to the sofa. She sat stiffly on the edge of the cushions, staring at her hands.

"Yeah, well, I'm sorry, too," Jim mumbled, not looking at her. The silence was penetrating. "And the answer is yes," he said in a louder voice. "I'm tired of fighting, too."

"What's happening to us, Jim?" Barbara whispered. "Are six years of marriage going to end in divorce because we can't resolve these differences, because we can't talk without fighting?"

"We're not going to get divorced, Barbara, for crying out loud!" Jim said defiantly. "My folks got divorced, but I'm just not going to. We'll work it out somehow, don't you worry."

"But how—*how*? I don't know what to do anymore. I don't know what to say. I went to college to be a business manager; I went to night school to learn about real estate; I even went to seminars to learn about makeup and hairstyling. But somehow I'm supposed to know automatically about marriage and sex and communication and housekeeping. It doesn't seem right, Jim. And it's not working very well."

Jim shifted restlessly in the rocker. "I guess we're supposed to learn those things from our parents or maybe through experience—I don't know. I sure didn't take any classes like that at college. I just learned about coaching and teaching."

"Well, see," Barbara said hesitantly, "that's why I thought we could learn a little about communication at this retreat.

The brochure said there are some easy steps to good communication in marriage, and they teach you how to do it during the weekend. Maybe it's a skill we can learn, just like anything else."

"Maybe. Do you still have the brochure?" Jim asked.

Barbara took it from the coffee table and handed it to him. She sat quietly while he read it.

"Hmmmm, it runs from Friday evening until Sunday noon. Doesn't cost very much. These people sound qualified to speak about it," Jim said as he read. "It says here that most couples talk only superficially or on an intellectual level. They never learn how to share their deeper needs or feelings. Because of that, conflict and disagreements occur that can't be resolved."

"It kind of sounds like us, don't you think?" Barbara asked.

"Yeah, maybe," Jim said, still reading. "We could learn skills of communicating on the deeper level, it says here, with many practical ways of continuing the communication at home. Well, it sounds pretty good, and the pastor's going to be there, too."

"And you like him, Jim," Barbara said eagerly. "That's what you've said."

"Yeah, he's a good guy. He's a real Vikings fan. I even heard him mention football in a sermon once!" Jim smiled as he remembered.

"And I'm sure there'll be other couples that we know from church," Barbara continued. "Jack and Sally, for instance. I know they're going. What do you think, Jim? Couldn't we give it a try? We couldn't lose anything. The resort where it's being held is very nice, and we'd get a weekend out of the city if nothing else." She looked anxiously at Jim, who was still studying the brochure.

"What do you think this means, Barbara—'sharing deeper needs or feelings'?" he asked. "That sounds like psychoanalysis or something a shrink would do."

"Well, I read once that marriage is the most intimate human relationship there is and that it's very healthy to tell your partner how you're feeling deep inside." Barbara chose her words carefully. "I find it hard to do that, probably because we never did it in my family, but there are times, Jim, when I really *want* to tell you what's happening inside me. Do you ever feel that way?"

"I guess so. It sounds risky though. I've always been afraid someone would make fun of me or tell everybody else how I felt. Maybe I started feeling that way when my dad left home. My mother told me I had to be the man of the house and that I had to be strong for her. I knew I couldn't cry or get mad about anything, because then she'd cry and cry."

"It sounds as if you learned to keep all your feelings inside," Barbara said.

"I guess that's right. And I've just never let them out except in football games or practice or when I do some boxing in the gym. I remember times when I've really pounded that punching bag!" Jim laughed a little.

"That's what happens sometimes when I play the piano," Barbara said, her eyes sparkling. "I can blow off so much steam just by playing a lot of *fortissimo!*"

Jim sighed and tapped the arm of the rocker with the brochure. "I hear your feelings coming out of the piano sometimes."

"Well?" Barbara asked again. "Couldn't we give it a try? Would it be OK if I called the president of the group and let her know we'd like to go?" She stood up in preparation to go to the phone.

Jim shook his head. "I don't know. I still think I should be here that weekend."

Barbara's expression tightened and her eagerness faded. "Oh, Jim, please don't say no. This retreat could change our whole marriage for the better."

"Oh, yeah?" Jim asked, tossing the brochure back on the coffee table. "I'm not so sure, but I'll think about it, OK?"

▪ Something to Talk About ▪

1. Describe the types of communication, positive and negative, that Barbara and Jim are experiencing in their marriage. Why aren't these forms of communication satisfactory?

2. Barbara and Jim feel unequipped and untrained for making a marriage work. What suggestions would you have for a couple planning to be married in regard to learning these skills? What suggestions do you have for Barbara and Jim now that they've been married six years and still feel inadequate?

3. Communication is the basis of any relationship. Marriage enrichment seminars and retreats usually show a couple that there are several levels of communication that become progressively deeper and more intimate. To begin, consider the following levels and note how they progress:

1. *The information-passing level.* This is surface conversation. "I have to work late tonight." "My sister phoned. Everything's OK on Jimmy's medical checkup." "The Scout council meeting is scheduled for Thursday." Even strangers can carry on conversations like this.
2. *The controlling, blaming, or "putting down" level.* A deeper, more intimate relationship exists because knowledge of past and current events is used. "You always act like a baby when we talk about money." "If you hadn't taken that new job, we wouldn't be in this mess now." "I'm not going to have sex with you tonight unless you apologize to me." Intimacy is used like a club for one's own benefit.
3. *The rational, intellectual level.* Deep conversations can take place. "The book I'm reading is fascinating. It describes human relationships. Let me explain them to you." "Now it seems to me that our biggest problem is our dissimilar backgrounds." Such conversations are interesting and thought-provoking but can keep barriers up between people.

4. *The honest, open, and vulnerable level.* Feelings are shared because trust exists. "I'm hurting inside. I feel like crying most of the time." "When we're together like this, I'm so happy, so much at peace." Deep and open communication occurs.

4. Find examples of all these communication levels in Barbara and Jim's story. Where do you see the beginnings of the fourth level? What seems to prompt this glimmer of deeper communication? Why do you think Jim seems afraid of deeper communication?

5. Based on what you've learned about communication and about Barbara and Jim, what do you think some results of the upcoming retreat could be for them?

6. Share personal examples of good or bad communication in marriage. How do these examples fit the levels of communication suggested above? How do the various experiences of communication affect a marriage relationship?

7. Christian marriage can be pictured in the imagery of Christ as the vine and husband and wife as the branches (see John 15:1-17). Draw a pencil sketch of the vine and branches. What becomes apparent about communication, sharing, and openness in a marriage like this?

2

▪ When a Couple Seeks ▪ Counseling

"Sit down and be comfortable, please," Dr. Matthews said, inviting Helene and Peter into her office. "I'm interested to hear how the exercise I gave you last week worked out."

Helene sat in a chair near the counselor's desk. Peter looked around and finally settled in the chair on the opposite side of the desk.

"It was a fiasco, if you really want to know," Helene said, crossing her legs and folding her arms. "He simply wouldn't cooperate."

"What?" Peter exploded. "*I* wouldn't cooperate? Doc, she's crazy! I did just what you suggested. I wrote down the problems that I see in our marriage, but she wouldn't agree that they're legitimate concerns."

"And he wouldn't agree with *my* list," Helene countered. "I very carefully detailed the biggest problems in our marriage, and he all but tore up the paper."

"Peter, do you feel you were not understood in explaining the problems?" the counselor asked.

"You bet I do! The biggest problem is her family. The next biggest problem is her obsession with her family," Peter said. "Her family takes all of her time."

"Oh, give me a break!" Helene said angrily. "Our biggest problem is that he's insanely jealous of the wonderful family I have. Now he's trying to punish me by flirting with the women at work!"

"All right, thank you," Dr. Matthews said. "We are beginning to rehash our first session together. I have another plan for today, and I'm going to need your cooperation to make it work. Can I count on that?" She looked at Helene and Peter, and they both nodded. Peter sighed, puffing his cheeks out as he exhaled. Helene recrossed her legs as she shifted in the chair.

"Good. I want to help you learn some good communication techniques in our counseling sessions so you can begin to help yourselves through your difficulties. One thing you will learn is that you cannot make intelligent, rational decisions or even have productive discussions until you know how the other person feels about the issue. Today we'll use our time in helping you learn about your partner's feelings in this matter of Helene's family. I want you to be honest and open in this room. I want you to forget about blaming the other person for anything," the counselor said. "You are to tell only about your own feelings and not anticipate the other person's feelings. Helene, will you start?"

She chewed on her lip. "I'm just to tell how I feel?"

"Yes, try to describe your inner feelings as best you can."

"Well," she hesitated, "I'm feeling lots of things. I'm afraid, for starters. I wake up in the morning with a huge pit in my stomach. I go to bed with the same feeling."

"Why do you feel that way?" the counselor asked.

"Because I'm afraid of losing my husband. I'm afraid my marriage is shot. I'm afraid of what's happening to our daughters," she said. "Also, I'm afraid for my parents. My mother's arthritis is getting worse, and my father has a heart condition. Neither of them is very well, and I'm trying to help them. You know what else I'm afraid of? I'm afraid my parents are going to die and I won't have done enough to help them. My mother especially. She likes to have things done a certain way. She always has. Nobody can please her like I can. Actually, I know I don't please her all the time either, but she says I'm the best." Helene smiled at the counselor.

"And how does that make you feel?" Dr. Matthews asked.

"Wonderful! She can make me feel so good about myself sometimes. I guess I work and work so I can hear her say that I'm the best," Helene said.

"You don't always feel good about yourself?" the counselor asked.

"No, not always. In fact, I usually don't," Helene answered. "I guess I feel pretty unhappy about myself most of the time. I've always felt that way, even as a kid. I knew I wasn't very good at things, and I made a lot of silly mistakes."

"How did you know that?" the counselor asked.

"Oh, my mother always told me," Helene said, nodding her head emphatically. "I tried very hard to make my mother happy by doing everything just the way she wanted it done. Then she'd relax, and everything would be good. Then she'd tell me I was the best."

"How do you think Peter feels hearing you say these things?" Dr. Matthews asked.

"I feel he doesn't understand why I go to my mother's house," Helene answered. "And I'm pretty confused and be-wildered about that. I don't understand why he objects when I want to spend time with my parents." Helene stared at her hands as she twisted her wedding ring around and around her finger. "Maybe he's mad because he never had a good home like I did, and that's why he won't let me enjoy mine."

"All right, Peter," Dr. Matthews said. "How are you feel-ing?"

Peter drummed his fingers on the desk. "Basically I guess I feel angry and frustrated. My wife spends so much time at her mother's house—cleaning, washing, ironing. *Our* house should look as good as theirs! It beats me why she even wants to be over there so much. I can't imagine being with my parents like that." Peter fished a cigarette out of his pocket and lit it. "My parents were always fighting. Things were a lot better when I wasn't there, so I just left when I was 17. Once in a great while I write them a letter, especially when something important happens like when our girls were born. My family's in Delaware, we're in Missouri—that's fine. I see them some-times, and I guess I do love them. How my wife can be with her parents so much is just beyond me. I feel left out."

"Why do you feel left out?" the counselor asked.

Peter blew the smoke out in a thin stream as he thought. "I'm disappointed. After my experience at home I always dreamed of having a secure, happy home and family. So I'm disappointed that I spend most of my time either at work or in my house alone. Even my daughters are at her mother's house. I'm left out." He drew on the cigarette, then quickly brushed a tear away with the back of his hand. "I'm *lonesome,* can't she see that? Sometimes I go from work over to the bar across the street with some of the women from the office. I do it just to have someone to talk to. And people seem to enjoy having me with them." Peter looked belligerently at his wife.

"And you don't have those feelings at home?" Dr. Matthews asked.

"No way! I'm lucky if anybody's even home when I get there. I'm basically a social kind of guy, Doc. I feel—I feel *betrayed* by my wife. She promised that she'd love and cherish me for as long as we live. I love her. The women at the office are OK, but I love my wife. She's the one I really want to be with. But I don't think she loves me. I really feel so alone." Peter crushed the cigarette in the ashtray and reached for his handkerchief. The tears had started rolling down his face, and his nose was running.

"I love you, Peter," Helene protested. She leaned forward in her chair. "Of course I do. How could you doubt that?"

Peter blew his nose. "I've been feeling that you love your mother more than me."

"Helene, would you like to respond to what you've just heard?" the counselor asked.

"I didn't know he felt that way," Helene said slowly. She turned to her husband. "I *do* love you, Peter, and I want a good home, too."

Dr. Matthews spoke as Helene and Peter tentatively looked at each other. "I hear you saying, Helene, that you feel your mother needs you. I hear Peter saying that he needs you. Also I hear you saying that you really do want to establish your own home. But you're caught between loyalties to two people. Is that how you feel?"

Helene sank back into her chair with a hopeless expression on her face. "Yes, I guess it is."

"And, Peter, I hear you saying you don't understand Helene's attachment to her mother and that you feel cheated that you have to share your wife with another person," the counselor said. "Is that how you feel?"

Peter looked at his wife. "That's it, Helene. That's how I feel."

"Well," Dr. Matthews said, "I think we've gone as far as we can go today. I suggest you continue to talk to each other at home about these feelings you've discovered. Next week we'll explore them further, and you will begin to make some decisions and plans based on what you've learned about your partner and yourself."

▪ Something to Talk About ▪

1. Describe what is happening in this counseling session. What does Helene learn about Peter? What does Peter learn about Helene?

2. What difference does it make when Helene and Peter share their honest feelings rather than blame and recriminations?

3. The counselor said, "One thing you will learn is that you cannot make intelligent, rational decisions or even have productive discussions until you know how the other person feels about the issue." What does this mean? What are some practical examples of this statement?

4. How did the counselor handle the session? What is the role of a marriage counselor? What is *not* the role of a counselor?

5. When is professional counseling desirable in a marriage? How bad should a situation get before it's brought to counseling? What can people realistically expect from marriage counseling?

6. If you have had any experience with marriage counseling, share your feelings and experiences.

7. What counseling resources are available in your church or community?

3

• When a Couple Copes •
with Two Careers

"Was Vince sure my car would be ready today?" Ann-Marie asked.

Paul checked the traffic to his left before pulling into the second lane. "That's what he said last night. The part he was waiting for finally came in yesterday, and the car should be ready by five this afternoon."

"Without my car I feel as if I'm stranded," Ann-Marie said. "Everyone at school has been great about giving me a lift home, but it's still a pain."

"I know, but I have to tell you, Ann-Marie, I've enjoyed this hour with you every morning this week." Paul reached over and took her hand, giving it a squeeze. "I'm going to miss your company next Monday."

Ann-Marie gave him a warm smile. "Me, too, Skip. I think we've talked more in this last week than we have for the past year."

"It sure gets my day off to a good start, being with you and talking," Paul said. "Even when the traffic is bad like it is today, I don't mind it because you're here." Red flashing lights far down the road indicated an accident or breakdown had occurred.

"That's one of the nicest things you've ever said to me," Ann-Marie laughed, "considering how much you hate Los Angeles traffic."

"Well, it's true. And you know what? It's made me think that we've got to continue this practice of talking every day." The traffic was at a standstill. Drivers were turning off their engines and getting out of their cars, stretching.

"What?" Ann-Marie said in alarm. "Are you saying I don't need my car?"

"No, no, of course not. We each need a car, and by tonight we'll have them both in running order," Paul soothed. "I just mean that we need to take time each day to visit the way we've been doing this week in the car. I've really enjoyed being able to share my feelings with you and hearing how you're doing."

"Oh, I agree. That part has been wonderful." Ann-Marie checked her watch. "Gosh, I wonder how long we're going to sit here. My teachers' meeting is scheduled for 8 A.M. It's 7:20 now."

"My first patient is scheduled for 8 A.M. too. I'm doing another root canal for Mrs. Carmichael. But I guess everyone will wait until we get there." Paul flashed his wife a quick smile. "Can't do anything about it when we're stuck like this."

Ann-Marie gazed out the side window at the cascade of ivy and bougainvillea flowing over the fence. "I really do love California, Skip. Look at those flowers. Aren't they glorious?"

Paul ducked his head so he could see the flowers. "I'll say. Usually I go by them so fast I don't even notice how pretty they are."

"That's kind of the way we live our lives," Ann-Marie said with a sigh. "Jamie and Kim are growing up so fast. Sometimes I don't think we appreciate them as much as we should. Sometimes I don't think we appreciate each other, either. This business of being a two-career family gets pretty frantic, what with the work and the house and the kids and—"

"But you know you love to teach, honey. Jamie and Kim are both in junior high with loads of activities, and between all of us we get the housework done somehow. I know you pretty well. You're a lot happier being back in teaching. And look at the wonderful promotion you got this year!"

"I know, and I am pleased about that. Did I tell you that Mr. Sullivan told me I'd be at the top of his list when I finish my school-adminstration classes? That means I could be a principal within a year or two!" Ann-Marie hugged her notebooks to herself, smiling.

"That's wonderful!" Paul began to move the car slowly forward as the traffic crept toward the cluster of red lights. The stop-and-start activity occupied his full attention. Ann-Marie began marking her language-arts papers.

"Oh, by the way, Ann-Marie, did I tell you that Ross called me a couple days ago?" Paul asked.

"Ross Allison? Your friend from dental school?"

"That's right. He had kind of an interesting idea—even an offer of sorts."

"An offer? What sort of offer?" Ann-Marie frowned a little.

"Well, he's always been interested in world missions in the church. Now he's putting a team together to go to Africa. It's a group of medical personnel who would spend time in a number of mission fields. He was just wondering if I'd like to be a part of something like that." Paul moved the car carefully past the flashing red lights and the tow trucks. Two cars had collided, and glass was being swept off the road by highway workers.

Ann-Marie looked at Paul with disbelief. "You mean go to Africa and work a few months?"

"Well, I guess it's more of a commitment than that, actually. Ross says he's looking for Christian doctors, dentists, and nurses to spend six to eight years in those mission fields."

Ann-Marie stared through the windshield at the congested traffic. "You're not—are you thinking about doing it?"

"I'm not thinking anything right now, honey. It's just an idea and—sort of an offer. That's all."

"Skip, this is something I've worried about for a long time."

"What? Going to the mission field?" Paul glanced at his wife who continued to look straight ahead.

"Just the whole business of moving to another place. I know it sounds selfish but what would happen to *my* career if you were to take another position? Or what if I got a terrific offer from some other school district? Here in L.A. it doesn't matter too much because we can commute, but what would happen if it were in another state or across the country? Or across the world?" Ann-Marie looked at her husband, who was concentrating on the road. "Am I making any sense at all?"

"Sure, I guess so. This never has been a problem before. You didn't have a career at stake until the last few years. I've just always assumed that you'd pick up everything and move wherever my work takes me. But I see you'd feel differently now." Paul's voice sounded disappointed.

"Oh, gosh, now I feel like an ogre," Ann-Marie said, looking away.

"No, no. It's only right that we look at this from all sides. I must admit that I didn't consider this part of it when I was talking to Ross. We just talked about the dental work that I'd do, and I somehow figured that you and the kids would come along and enjoy the excitement of living in a foreign country. That wasn't very realistic of me," Paul said.

Ann-Marie sighed. "I wouldn't even give this much thought except that I know you've always wanted to serve in foreign missions. Your mother has told me that you dreamed about it when you were a boy. Now here comes a chance for you to make your dream come true, and I become a problem."

"You're not a problem," Paul assured her, reaching over to grasp her arm. "It wasn't a realistic idea for us, and I'll just forget about it. Your work in the school and all the opportunities you have are too important for you to leave."

"I have tenure now too," Ann-Marie offered.

"Right. And it would be selfish of me to demand that you give that up. And it would also be selfish to expect the kids to leave their friends and schools and activities." Paul drove off the freeway and into the proper exit lane. "We're going to be on time after all, honey."

"Good. I really need to be at that meeting," Ann-Marie said, watching the traffic sweep along. After a few moments she exclaimed, "I feel terrible!"

"Why?" Paul said, quickly glancing at her. "What's wrong? Are you sick?"

"No, no. I feel terrible about throwing a wet blanket on your dream like that. And I feel like I'm against God or something."

"What?" Paul drove through the last intersection, nearing the school.

"Well, it's bad enough that I can't wholeheartedly enjoy the idea of going to the mission field, but there's another dimension here. We're talking about *God's* work being done through you, and when I oppose it, I'm opposing God. That really does make me feel guilty and terrible."

Paul pulled into the school parking lot and stopped the car. "Believe me, you don't have to feel that way. It was a harebrained idea, and my family's happiness is much more important to me than working with Ross." He leaned over and kissed Ann-Marie.

She got out of the car, taking her briefcase and purse. "Bye, Skip. Thanks. See you at dinner time." Ann-Marie slowly walked into the school and her classroom. Someone had drawn a big heart on the chalkboard. Inside was written, "We love Mrs. Skippels."

▪ Something to Talk About ▪

1. Describe the relationship Ann-Marie and Paul have. What levels of communication do you find in their marriage? Describe their careers and their feelings about them. How are they managing careers, home, and family?

2. Describe the offer Paul received from Ross and his response to it. Describe Ann-Marie's reaction to this news and her response. What do you think will happen in this family regarding the offer? What do you think *should* happen? When should an individual give up his or her own dreams to allow the partner's dreams to be fulfilled? What pressures and influences are at work in this particular situation?

3. What if Paul's job offer was to a prestigious clinic in Seattle where he could triple his income? What if Ann-Marie were offered a state education-consultant position in Sacramento involving much prestige? What if Paul or Ann-Marie actually lost his or her position and a move was required to find work?

4. What pressures occur in two-career families? Which ones do you find described in this story? How can a couple ease these pressures? What sacrifices may the couple be called on to make?

5. Describe any experiences you may have had in regard to a two-career marriage, or in regard to "giving up" dreams for the sake of a partner. What positive and/or negative results occurred?

6. In larger or smaller ways, all married couples must sacrifice for each other. How can loving sacrifice be prevented from becoming subservient martyrdom or humiliating deprivation? How can graceful receiving be prevented from becoming continuous expectation or angry taking? What guideline for Christian marriage is found in Jesus' words in Matt. 10:39: "Whoever finds his life will lose it, and whoever loses his life for my sake will find it"?

4

▪ When the Children ▪ Leave Home

Phil came into the house for his coffee at 10 A.M. Doris took the sweet rolls out of the oven and frosted them. "Here you go, Phil. Hot and sticky—just the way you like them."

"Mmmmmm, wonderful!" Phil smiled at his wife and then picked up the morning paper. "Anything new happen?"

"Everything's about the same, thank goodness," Doris replied, pouring herself some coffee and sitting down at the table with Phil. "I guess the Marines are just cruising around the Mediterranean, acting as a deterrent."

"After that last incident in Lebanon, we have to hope that everyone over there has the good sense to keep the peace." Phil leafed through the paper, glancing at the headlines.

"I think about Tim all the time," Doris said, sipping her coffee. "I can hardly imagine our little boy as a Marine."

"He's done right well—a farm boy from Wisconsin finishing at the top of his class in that rigorous Marine training."

"Oh, I'm proud of his accomplishments, but I worry so much about him, Phil. I worry about him getting injured or killed—that's the worst. But I also worry about the influence the military life will have on him. And I worry about—"

"I know, I know," Phil interrupted. "But worrying doesn't do any good. Tim wanted to join the Marines, and now he's one of them."

"I had so hoped he'd go to the university like Jane did. And that's another thing—I can't stop thinking about Jane either." Doris gazed sadly at her husband, who was consuming his third sweet roll.

"Why worry about her?" Phil asked. "She's married and all settled in Green Bay."

"Oh, it just doesn't seem right for her to be married to—that man."

"Well, he isn't the one we wanted for her, but that can't be helped. She's so crazy in love with Al that she married him, despite the differences in their backgrounds. Well, I can't sit here all morning. I've got to get that tractor fixed so I can plow tomorrow." Phil stood up and took one last swallow of coffee.

"I'm thinking of taking a little trip to Green Bay," Doris said offhandedly.

Phil turned from the doorway to look at her. "You're what?"

"I just thought I'd hop on the bus and go see Jane."

"You're crazy! They've been married only two weeks and are barely back from their honeymoon. Leave them alone. Besides, I need you here." Phil left the house and headed for the toolshed.

Doris stared at the door, the tears welling up in her eyes. He just didn't understand, that was all. He didn't understand how empty her life was without Tim and Jane. Phil was always so busy with the farm and what did *she* have? Now that the kids were both gone, her life was so—meaningless.

Phil's last words rattled around in Doris' head as she cleaned up the dishes. "I need you here," he had said. "I need you here." *Sure, he needs me to be his slave. He surely doesn't need me for anything else,* she thought bitterly. All they ever talked about was the farm or the kids. He ate his meals and slept in their bed, that was about it. The tears slipped down her face as Doris covered the rest of the sweet rolls. She felt so lonesome, so empty.

At 3:30 P.M. Phil came into the house for his afternoon snack. It was very quiet, but he found coffee in a thermos and several pieces of chocolate cake on a plate. Where was Doris? he wondered. For a moment he panicked. Did she take off for Green Bay after all? Then he found the note tucked under the plate: "Have gone to my circle meeting. Back by 5 P.M. or so."

Phil sighed in relief and settled at the table to enjoy the cake and coffee. Wow, if Doris had gone to Green Bay—he needed her so much. Now that the kids were both gone, things were so different. Tim cruising around over there in the Mediterranean—anything could happen to his son. Part of Phil was on that ship with Tim. And Jane with her new husband in Green Bay. Phil had seen a mean streak in that fellow that he didn't like. Once he'd watched Al tease an old dog unmercifully. What if he treated Jane like that?

Savoring the rich chocolate cake, Phil reflected on himself. Doris was his mainstay, his rock. What would he ever do without her? She gave him meaning and purpose in life. But things were so different now, with the kids gone. Doris had even begun to change. Phil poured more steaming coffee from the thermos. He wondered what to do for Doris, to help her. He wondered about himself, how he, too, was changing. When the kids were little, everything was right with the world. They had loved the farm, with all the animals and the wide open spaces in which to run and play. Phil ached inside as he thought of Tim confined to a ship and Jane confined to an apartment. Sometimes the pain was so bad he had to escape it. After drinking the coffee rapidly and burning his tongue, Phil left the house. The cows would soon need to be milked.

When dinner was over and the dishes put away, the late TV news was beginning. Doris came into the family room to find

Phil dozing in his chair. "Wake up, Phil. The news is coming on."

Phil jerked to attention, suddenly wide awake. The lead story was about a new battle in Beirut. Several Marines had been injured. And now an American troop ship was on its way to join the Marines stationed there.

"Oh, dear God!" Doris cried. "That must be Tim's ship. He's going to Beirut."

Phil shushed her, trying to hear the rest of the story. But the newscaster was already talking about a bill the president had vetoed. "Now, Doris, we don't know for sure that it's Tim's ship. It could be another one, you know." But his face was tight with anxiety.

"It's like my worst dream," Doris moaned, pacing and wringing her hands. "And there's nothing we can do."

"Nothing except pray for him." Phil was frozen in his chair but the words spilled out of him. "Doris, I've been thinking a lot today. I had a premonition something like this was happening. Come here, sit with me."

Doris crawled into Phil's lap and hugged him. He wrapped his arms around her. "Lord Jesus, we're scared," Phil said in a thick voice. "Be with our Tim and all the other Marines on that ship. We pray that he'll be safe. We love him so much."

Doris wept quietly into Phil's shirt. His tears dampened her hair. They held each other very closely.

"Doris, when I couldn't find you here this afternoon, I thought maybe you'd gone to Green Bay after all. I couldn't stand it if you left me, even for a little while. I need your strength and your presence right with me."

"And my sweet rolls and chocolate cake?" Doris asked in a muffled voice.

"Well, they're OK too," Phil said, laughing a little. "But it's you I need, you know. When we had the kids with us all the time, I didn't think about it much, but now that they're gone, I realize that it's you who makes the difference in my life."

Doris leaned back so she could see into Phil's eyes. "I've been feeling very lonesome, Phil. People talk about the 'empty nest,' and I'm beginning to understand what that means. And I've been feeling that you were so busy you didn't know I was here."

Phil hugged her even closer. "You've got to be kidding! You're *everything* to me. I guess I've been working hard just to—just to kind of forget about Tim and Jane being away. But you, you're my whole life."

Doris snuggled close to her husband. She felt warm and safe in his arms. "You know what, Phil? This is almost like when we were first married. Those two years when we didn't have the kids—remember how special that time was?"

"Of course I remember. But there's one big difference— we're even closer now. The kids are on their own, and it's just you and me." Phil smoothed Doris' hair.

They were quiet for a while, enjoying the closeness of each other. Doris broke the silence. "Kathy said something interesting today at my circle meeting, Phil. She was talking about her kids and how they're away now too. And she said that she has 'relinquished' them to the Lord. Isn't that an interesting thought?"

"Hmmmm," Phil said, pondering. "Relinquished. Did she say how she did that?"

"She said she prayed to the Lord, saying she'd done all she could for the boys at this time and that they were gone from home. Then she asked the Lord to take care of them, to work his will in their lives, and to give her the peace of knowing that he was holding them and caring for them. Kathy said she prays that prayer every day, and that she has a lot of peace. And she's starting to find her own life now."

Phil gently pushed Doris from his lap, helping her to stand. He, too, got to his feet and turned off the TV. "Come on, Doris. We're going for a walk."

"What? Why?" Doris looked at Phil in amazement. "Where?"

"We're going out in the apple orchard and take a stroll," Phil said. "And while we're at it, we're going to do some relinquishing of our own."

The door softly closed behind them. Phil took Doris' hand, and together they walked toward the bent, sweet-smelling trees. The moonlight created a luminous pathway for them.

▪ Something to Talk About ▪

1. Doris and Phil are beginning a new phase in their marriage, one which is sometimes described as the "empty nest." Describe their circumstances. How does Doris feel? How does Phil feel?

2. How are Doris and Phil communicating? Describe the various types of communication they experience in the story. In what ways did they take each other for granted? In what ways did they assume they knew what the other person was thinking and feeling? How can a couple avoid these pitfalls?

3. What does it mean to relinquish one's children or loved ones to the Lord? Does such relinquishment mean that parents are no longer concerned? What difference will it make in Doris and Phil's attitude to relinquish Tim and Jane to the Lord? What do you think Kathy meant when she said she was "starting to find her own life now"?

4. If you have experienced the empty nest, describe how you coped with it. What joys and/or frustrations did it bring?

5. What suggestions do you have for Phil and Doris as they enter this new phase of their marriage? What glimmers of the future do you find in the story?

5

• When a Couple's Friends •
Are Being Divorced

Carla was looking at the clock every five minutes. It was
11:14 P.M., and Al still hadn't come home. He'd eaten dinner
with the family but then had gone out, saying he had to meet
a client. Carla hadn't thought anything of it at the time, knowing he'd received a telephone call at 6:30 P.M. But it seemed
strange that a meeting with a client would take this long.

The kids were all in bed, and Carla loaded the dishwasher.
After turning the machine on, she closed the draperies and
locked the doors. It was 11:30 P.M.

Carla put on her nightgown and set her hair. Her heart was
beating rapidly. Maybe Al had had car trouble. Maybe the
client had taken him to a bar. Or maybe Al wasn't with a client
at all.

At midnight Carla turned out the light and got into bed,
but it was impossible to sleep with her heart thumping and
her stomach feeling like a deep pit. She lay rigidly in the queen-
size bed, wondering what to do. Should she just lie here and
try to sleep? Should she call the police on the off chance there'd
been an accident? Or should she start to be realistic and face
what she was thinking?

Carla got out of bed and turned the light on again. Going into the living room, she peered around the draperies. No car out in front, and no car lights moving along the street. She sat in the big armchair in the dark, trying to sort out her thoughts.

Ever since Alice had told her that Kevin had left and she was getting a divorce, Carla had become suspicious of Al's activities. It wasn't that she noticed anything new about Al. It was just that if *Kevin* had been seeing other women—Kevin who seemed to be such a devoted husband, Kevin who had lived next door for eight years and seemed more like a brother—if Kevin could have left Alice, then anything was possible. And Carla had started noticing how strange some of Al's stories seemed. Like tonight—who had that phone call been from anyway? Al had hurried to answer it so no one had heard the voice on the other end. Was it really a client? Or was it a girlfriend? Maybe it was Al's secretary pretending to set up a client visit but really setting up a rendezvous with Al for herself.

Carla began visualizing the two of them together. She never had liked that woman. She probably had had her eyes on her boss all this time.

The sound of the key in the front door startled Carla, and she jumped up. Al's eyes squinted from the sudden light Carla turned on in the hall.

"Where have you been, Al?" Carla demanded. "Do you realize it's nearly 1 A.M.?"

"I had a flat tire." Al's voice was tired and he was out of sorts. "I left the office at 10, but I had to take my client to his hotel, and then I got the flat out on the freeway. I didn't think I'd ever get home." He showed her his dirty hands before going into the bathroom to wash.

Carla stood in the hallway. Part of her was relieved, but part of her was still suspicious. A flat tire? That was the oldest story in the book. Was he telling the truth, or was it just a ruse? He could have dirtied his hands to make his story seem real. After a few moments Carla turned off the lights and went to bed. Al was already in his pajamas, crawling into bed himself.

"Goodnight," he said, turning to face the wall.

"Goodnight," she said, staring at the ceiling. He hadn't even kissed her.

Carla prepared scrambled eggs for breakfast. The children were off to school by 8 A.M., but Al lingered over his coffee and newspaper. This was Wednesday, the day he usually left to visit the two company branches in the southern part of the state.

"Will you be back early on Friday?" Carla asked.

"Probably," Al replied, deep in the sports page.

"Bill has a basketball game at 4:30 Friday afternoon. He'd like to have you there if you can make it."

"I'll have to see."

Carla stared at her husband for a moment. She decided she couldn't let him leave for two days without saying something. "Al, where were you last night?"

"What do you mean, where was I?" Al glanced at Carla, then back at the paper.

"Just what I said. Where were you?"

Her tone of voice brought Al's full attention to the conversation. "I was at the office, I told you. Then I had that blasted flat tire. What's with this inquisition?"

"I suppose I can call the office to see if you really were there?"

"What? Of course not. Everyone was gone but the janitors. What are you implying? Don't you believe me?" Al's eyes were flashing angry sparks. The sports page was forgotten.

"No, actually I don't, Al. I've been wondering for some time if you're seeing a girlfriend on the sly. Last night just seemed too perfect to me." Carla's words were cold.

Al stood up, threw the paper on the floor and stared unbelievingly at his wife. "You're crazy! You're just *crazy*!"

"Am I? Is that what Kevin said to Alice?"

Al's jaw dropped in amazement. He closed his mouth and rubbed his hand across it, then began pacing around the little dining area. "You think—I mean, just because our neighbors—you think I'm running around." And suddenly Al began to laugh. He howled until the tears ran down his cheeks. He pointed at Carla, he pointed toward Kevin's house, he pointed at himself wordlessly, the great peals of laughter preventing him from saying anything.

Carla watched him suspiciously, but finally she, too, had to laugh, if not at the situation then at her husband. He made a very funny picture, and the laughter was contagious.

Al sat down at the table and wiped his face and eyes with his napkin. Little giggles were still coming out of him, but he could finally talk. "Carla, baby, that has got to be the funniest thing I've ever heard. To think you suspect *me* of running around with some young thing. You flatter me, sweetheart! To think that you think—" and the laughter burbled out of Al once again.

Carla was feeling silly. The laughter had taken the hurt and fear out of her, and the whole thing seemed funny. It *was* hard to imagine Al with anybody else. Suddenly she saw him as the man she'd known and loved for 20 years. These days he was losing his hair and sported quite a few extra pounds. Let's face it, both of them were aging, but Kevin was aging, too.

Al leaned on the breakfast table, finally in control of himself. "Now listen, Carla. I'm awfully sorry I didn't call last night, but I took it for granted that you'd be sleeping, and I didn't want to worry you. But it seems to me that last night isn't really the important thing anyway. It's this whole stupid situation with Kevin and Alice's divorce."

"Yes, and with Ronnie and Marcia, and with Jerry and Ruthanne," Carla reminded him.

"Right. Lately it's seemed as if our friends' and neighbors' marriages are collapsing all around us. I'll bet you've been talking to Alice a lot, haven't you?"

"Well, of course. She lives right next door, she's my good friend, and she's miserable."

"And you've been hearing all sorts of terrible stories about Kevin, which is natural. Look, honey, I'm not Kevin, and I'm not Ronnie or Jerry either. I *love* you. I'm not going to run off, believe me. I wonder, has it occurred to you that Kevin may have talked to me about Alice?"

Carla's eyes widened. "Did he? When? What did he say?"

"He called me at the office one day, and we had lunch. I'm not going to repeat everything he said, because it was personal, but you should realize that the problems in that marriage are not entirely Kevin's. Alice hasn't been perfectly straight with you if she's saying that it's all Kevin's fault."

Carla looked a little uncertain. "Well, she didn't exactly say it was all his fault, but she told me plenty about his sneaking around."

"See, there you go. You're beginning to transfer Alice's suspicions about Kevin over to me. Carla, I've never been unfaithful to you, and I'm not fooling around now." Al looked at Carla slyly. "How about *you*? Are you running around with some gorgeous hunk while I'm away on my business trips?"

"Al!" Carla was horrified. "How can you *say* such a thing?"

Al started laughing again. "I couldn't resist, I couldn't resist! But you looked the way I felt when you accused me."

Carla went around the table and gave Al a big hug. "You've made your point, you clown. I love you with all my heart."

"I love *you*, you crazy woman! But seriously, I think we've got to talk this out very carefully. I'm beginning to feel as if we're the last married couple in town, and that's scary. Maybe we should be finding some ways to strengthen the good marriage we've got."

Carla kissed her husband. "We need a lot more time to talk things over, Al."

"Tell you what. Next week I have to go to Denver for the corporation convention. See if Mrs. Kelly can stay with the kids so you can come with me. We'd have four days to talk and enjoy each other."

▪ Something to Talk About ▪

1. Carla is feeling many different emotions. Describe them. Describe Al's feelings. In what ways do we take our spouses for granted? When is it good to be that comfortable? When is it a problem? What can be done about it?

2. If you've had close friends or relatives share their problems with separation and divorce with you, describe how you felt. In what ways did their comments alter your feelings about your own marriage and partner? Were your feelings changed for the better or for the worse?

3. Why do you think divorces seem to be "contagious" within groups of friends or neighbors?

4. What advice would you give Carla and Al or any couple whose friends are being divorced?

5. Notice the types of communication or noncommunication that took place between Carla and Al. Carefully check each phase of the story to discover the various forms, both verbal and nonverbal. Do they look familiar to you? How do they help or hinder a marriage relationship?

6. What role does humor and laughter play in communication? in marriage? Describe what happened when laughter suddenly burst forth during the tense breakfast.

7. What experiences or methods can you recommend that would strengthen a marriage? If you have taken part in any marriage-strengthening experience, share how it helped you.

8. In what ways can the church help couples strengthen their marriages?

6

▪ When Difficulties Arise ▪
with Parents
or Parents-in-Law

"Mommy's mad," Tammy announced when Bill entered the house. The seven-year-old watched her father to see what he would do with this bit of information.

Bill glanced at Tammy as he pulled off his greasy coveralls. "Oh? What's she mad about?"

"Grandma got mommy fired from her job," Tammy said, pointing toward the kitchen. "Mommy says we're going to leave this stupid town."

Bill hung up his coveralls and tossed his boots in the closet. "Well, I don't think we'll be leaving before dinner anyway. Why don't you go play with Tad while I talk to your mother?" Tammy hesitated but finally went to find her brother.

Bill washed his hands in the laundry room sink. His heart was pounding. A guy could leave his house in the morning with things relatively peaceful and return at night to discover that everything had blown apart. What on earth had his mother done now? He knew JoAnn loved her work at the gift shop. Was it possible that his wife no longer had the job?

One step into the kitchen was enough to convince Bill that Tammy had told the truth about one thing anyway—JoAnn was mad. Everything from her angry stance at the stove to the slamming of the cupboard door to the crashing of the frying pan in the sink signaled very heavy weather. "Hi, honey," he said as casually as possible. "Something sure smells good." JoAnn shot him a malevolent look. "Well, I guess I'll just check the sports page before dinner." Bill hastily left the war zone and settled into his chair in the den, heaving a great sigh. Maybe this would just blow over.

Dinner was a disaster. Tammy and Tad picked at their food, giggling to each other. Bill tried to start a conversation but met an icy wall when JoAnn refused to speak a word. Finally Bill picked up the sports page and read his favorite column as he shoveled in the spaghetti.

Bill heard the bedroom door slam about 7:30 P.M. He tried to concentrate on the movie on TV but finally gave it up as a bad job. Bill turned off the TV and headed for the bedroom. He hated to do it, but he was going to have to face the problem head-on.

JoAnn lay rigidly on the bed, staring at the wall. Bill slowly sat down beside her and gently rubbed her back. Neither of them spoke. Then Bill could feel her body begin to shake. JoAnn was sobbing. He stretched out beside her and held her closely. The sobs subsided after what seemed like an eternity and JoAnn turned to grab a tissue.

"I hate her," JoAnn said hoarsely. Her nose was stopped up so her words sounded as if they came from a deep hole. "Why can't she leave me alone? I swear she's out to destroy me."

Bill continued to hug his wife. He didn't know what to say. Suddenly she sat up and faced him.

"Bill, I can't live in this town any longer. I've put up with this garbage from your mother for over 10 years, and I've had it. Nothing I do pleases her, and lately she's been getting vicious. Do you know what she did to me today?" Bill shook his head. "She came into the store while I was gone for lunch and she told my boss that she knew for a fact I was stealing items from the store. That witch said I gave them away for Christmas presents and that she herself had seen the tags on the items, proving they were from Gifts Galore." JoAnn blew her nose and threw the tissue on the bed. "Do you know what happened then? My boss fired me the minute I came back. He didn't even ask me for my side of the story. He didn't even *ask*! Your mother had so completely convinced him I was guilty that all he did was yell at me with her accusations, and then he ordered me out of the store. He said he'd send two weeks' severance pay but only because he had to. I don't have my job anymore, Bill. Your mother *maliciously* and *viciously* took it away from me." JoAnn began to cry once again, beating the bed with her fists. "I *hate* her! I want to leave this town! I want to go away!"

Bill sat up and patted his wife on the back as she sobbed. *Good grief, what am I going to do now?* he wondered. *My mother really went too far this time.* Bill knew she'd hurt JoAnn before, but *this*! It was hard to believe.

"Well?" JoAnn demanded, sitting up and wiping her eyes. "What are you going to do about it? Are you my husband or your mother's little boy?"

"Wait a minute," Bill said, drawing back. "Don't start aiming at me! *I* didn't do anything."

"That's just the trouble, Bill. You haven't done anything— not one thing!" JoAnn's voice was stronger. "I have had to take your mother's bad temper and accusations for 10 years, and you've never done anything about it. She hated me right from the beginning, and you never stood up for me."

"Well, I married you, didn't I? That showed her that I loved you."

"Yes, of course, but we had to elope to do it," JoAnn reminded him. "There was no way you were going to face the problems she'd give us if we tried to have a nice church wedding here in town. And then when we got back from our honeymoon, she'd completely furnished our apartment, saying that my taste was all in my mouth and that no son of hers would live in the pigpen I was sure to create. You never said a word about that."

"JoAnn, I've learned over the years how to handle my mother. I don't rile her up."

"Your definition of 'not riling her up' is to sit back and let her do whatever she wants to do," JoAnn shouted. "Even when she invites us to dinner and prepares a meal loaded with cheese, you don't say anything. You know and *she* knows I'm highly allergic to cheese. I can't even stay in the dining room because of the strong odor. And what about the times she's come to the children's school conferences with the teachers? She has no business being there, but she won't listen to me. She *never* listens to me, because I'm a nonperson in her eyes. But she'd listen to *you* if you'd just be firm with her."

Bill rubbed his face with his hands. "You just don't understand. You don't know about this, even after all these years."

JoAnn watched her husband sink back on the bed, the picture of defeat. Her anger started to dissipate, and she sighed deeply. "Bill, I decided something this afternoon. I love you, but I won't be pushed around by your mother anymore. I know it sounds harsh, and I'm sorry, but you're going to have to make a choice."

Bill looked at her with alarm. Her tone of voice was too calm. "What choice are you talking about?"

"Either you're going to help me by standing up to your mother and making her stop this destructive activity in our lives or—" JoAnn stopped to take a deep breath. "Or I'm going to take Tad and Tammy and go to Baltimore. I know I can get a job there, and I can start a new life."

Bill couldn't believe his ears. He opened his mouth but no words came out. He gestured toward JoAnn and toward himself. Staring numbly he finally said, "I don't believe it. You can't. What will I do?"

"Listen to me," JoAnn said, sitting on the bed and taking his hands. "We've got to work together on this. I don't want to leave. What I want is to have you stand with me in solving this problem. Can't you do that, Bill?"

Bill searched JoAnn's eyes, trying to find courage and light there. He swallowed hard. "I want to do it, but I don't know how I can."

"I'll *help* you," JoAnn promised. "Our whole family and marriage rest on this, Bill. But you're going to have to stand up to your mother and tell her some things. Can you try to do that?"

"Well, will you go with me to do it?"

"Of course I will. We'll go together. Bill, I want my job back. Please, we've got to go to her tonight and tell her she must go back to Gifts Galore and tell my boss she made a mistake. Please! She'd do it for you if you said she had to." JoAnn pleaded with her words and her eyes.

"Gosh, I've never told her anything like that," Bill said, slowly standing. "Do you really think she'd listen to me?"

"She would if you meant it, honey. She won't risk losing you."

Bill thought a few moments, then raised his chin. "All right, let's do it. And while I'm there, I'm going to talk to her about the cheese."

JoAnn laughed and clapped her hands. "Bill, if we just let her know we won't tolerate her interference in our lives, we can begin a whole new chapter. It'll mean everything to our marriage and our family!"

"You know, I feel better already." Bill opened the bedroom door. "If you're by my side, if we're together, we can do anything."

Tammy and Tad stood in the hallway. "Are you going to tell grandma to get lost, dad?" Tammy asked.

Bill laughed, hugging JoAnn. "No, I'm just going to tell her that we won't let her make us unhappy anymore. And your mother and I are going to do it together."

▪ Something to Talk About ▪

1. Describe Bill and JoAnn as individuals—their personalities, their feelings. Describe their marriage and their relationship.

2. What major step have Bill and JoAnn taken in this crisis? What effect will this step have on their marriage? on their relationship with his mother?

3. Bill's mother undoubtedly will not stop her interference after just one confrontation. What further steps will probably have to be taken by this couple?

4. If you have had a difficult experience with parents or parents-in-law, describe the situation and how you coped with it. What specific steps did you take? What steps do you think *should* have been taken?

5. Relationships with parents and parents-in-law should be that of supportive friends. If you've experienced or know of relationships like this, describe them. What made the relationships work?

6. In a marriage, where does one's first priority belong? What priority follows next? Where do parents and parents-in-law occur in the list of priorities?

7. Jesus said to the Pharisees when questioned about divorce, "Haven't you read . . . that at the beginning the Creator 'made them male and female,' and said, 'For this reason a man will leave his father and mother and be united to his wife, and the two will become one flesh'? So they are no longer two, but one. Therefore what God has joined together, let man not separate" (Matt. 19:4-6). What implications does this passage have for Bill and JoAnn? for any married couple? What guidelines does it give a couple in dealing with any situation?

7

▪ When a Couple Retires ▪

Settled behind his old rolltop desk, Sid carefully wrote a personal check to his nephew, Michael Wheeler. Lila peered over his shoulder as he filled in the amount. "Wowee, Sid! You're going to give Mike a thousand dollars? What in the world are you up to?"

"Lila, Mike is going to be 35 years old on Sunday. That's a very important birthday for him in terms of his retirement plans." Sid waved the check in the air to dry the ink. "I know for a fact that Mike is spending all his money on his family and that he hasn't started any kind of retirement fund. Don't you remember that we started saving for retirement when we were in our 30s?"

Lila sat in the armchair beside the desk. "Yes, I do remember. It was rough going, salting away those dollars."

"But look how important it is for us now that we're retired. Lila, it's the money invested in one's 30s and 40s that makes a financial base for retirement. The interest on that money accumulates to a staggering amount."

"Well, I've never understood all that financial jargon, but I do know that between our Social Security, your pension, and the savings account we worked on for all those years, we have a very comfortable retirement. That's a real good idea for a gift, Sid. But are you sure we can afford it?"

Sid took an envelope from a drawer and carefully inserted the check in it. "Yes, I'm sure we can afford it. Besides, Mike is my brother Earl's only child. If Earl and Martha were alive, they'd be helping Mike, so I feel responsible to do something substantial." He started licking the flap on the envelope.

"Wait, Sid, don't seal it yet," Lila said. "If we're going to give Mike a financial gift for retirement, I think we should also give him something else."

"Like what?"

"Like a letter to put in the envelope along with the check. You and I have talked about retirement for so long and we've observed so many of our friends retire, that we know quite a bit about it. Remember how you've always said that a person has to learn to retire just as much as he or she has to learn to work? Why don't we share some of our ideas about preparing for retirement with Mike and Carolyn? They probably won't fully recognize the value of those ideas yet, but it'll give them a head start on thinking about it anyway."

Sid chuckled and leaned over to pat Lila's knee. "You've done it again, sweetheart. You've put the frosting on the cake. OK, what shall we say in the letter?" Sid looked expectantly at Lila, his pencil poised to take notes.

"Let's begin by wishing him a happy birthday, of course, and let him know the money is meant for a retirement investment. Tell him your theory about having to learn to retire."

"OK, and then we need to point out that everyone has to have a purpose in retirement, just as they do in their working years." Sid wrote as he talked.

"Right. Be sure to tell them how we volunteer our time in the children's hospital. Tell them how we look forward to our days in the playroom and how we help feed the little ones."

"Lila, I can't get all of that in a letter. We can tell them the details later. Now we want to tell them about the importance of developing hobbies." Sid wrote his notes quickly, jotting down the thoughts that were rushing through his mind.

"Oh, yes. Tell them about your ham radio shack and my ceramics. Tell them how we square dance and how we've done it for years and years." Lila couldn't sit still when she thought about dancing. She twirled around the room.

"Come on, twinkle toes," Sid said, "we've got to finish this letter. I want to type it up this morning."

Lila planted a big kiss on Sid's balding head before she sat in the armchair again. "And tell them how important it is to stay involved in their church. I know Mike and Carolyn are really busy there now, but tell them to keep it up. Tell them why, Sid. Then close the letter with more birthday greetings."

As Lila washed the breakfast dishes and planned dinner, she could hear Sid's typewriter clattering. There'd be long pauses of silence, then the typing would resume with new intensity. After an hour, Sid appeared with the letter.

"There, I finished it. You know, Lila, it was interesting to put our retirement ideas down on paper. I've never seen them written out before."

A host of little elves and fairies had materialized on the breakfast table. Lila was preparing to paint some of her ceramic creations.

"Are we different, Sid? I mean, do you think we look at retirement differently from most people?" Lila carefully painted an elf's eyes and nose.

"Yes, I think we do. I talk to some of my friends, and they're having a lot of financial difficulties. I asked Ralph one day about his financial setup, and I was horrified. I come from a family who always looked ahead to retirement, but I'm finding that most people don't think much about it. Certainly they don't think about it when they're young. Ralph said he didn't start a retirement account until he was 52. By then his prime years for earning interest on his savings were long gone. I've decided that money problems are the biggest cause of dissat-isfaction in retirement."

"Oh, Sid, I think the biggest problems are relationships and expectations. For instance, Vera tells me that her husband doesn't want her to go out to lunch with her friends now that he's retired. He wants to do everything she does and go every-where she goes. He wants her all to himself."

Sid laughed. "Wouldn't you love it if I went everywhere you did?" Lila glared at him. "That's what I meant when I told Mike that it's necessary to have a purpose in retirement. Did you tell Vera about our calendar?"

"I surely did. I told her how we respect each other's time and plans, and how we write everything down on the calendar, even the dates we make to do things together. She could hardly believe it. Said something about how retirement should mean not having to live by a calendar, but she looked envious when I talked about my Women's Club luncheon dates and my work on the auxiliary board at church. I just told her we had agreed a long time ago that we wouldn't stifle each other in retirement. Read me the letter you wrote to Mike."

"Oh, sure," Sid said, adjusting his glasses.

Dear Mike,

Congratulations and best wishes on your 35th birthday. We feel this is an important milestone in your life and it is our privilege to help you mark it. We know that retirement sounds a long way off to you right now, but believe us when we say that your birthdays will go by mighty fast. It was when we were 35 that we started investing seriously in our retirement, and we want to start you and Carolyn on the same road. We give you this money to invest in an Individual Retirement Account (IRA) or another high-interest sav-ings program. We only ask that you continue to put money away in the account on a regular basis, providing a strong financial base for your retirement.

Also we want to suggest some other things that will be enjoyable now and will help in your retirement. First, remember that you have to learn to retire just as much as you had to learn to work. And learning to retire is a long process, one that begins now with your financial plans and with your pastimes and hobbies. There are even classes and seminars you can take that will help you make plans and adjust your thinking.

Secondly, become aware right now that you will always need a purpose in your lives. You'll shrivel up and waste away without goals and purposes in retirement, just as you would right now. Your involvement with other people is not only helpful for them but is essential for your own well-being. As you know, we both volunteer our time at the children's hospital, something that brings us much joy.

Thirdly, be sure that both you and Carolyn develop hobbies right now that will be of interest to you when you retire. Our lives have been enriched because of the ham radio operation and the ceramics. We also enjoy square dancing together and have traveled to many programs and conventions where we've met such wonderful people.

And finally, continue your involvement in your church. It is only through your relationship to the Lord that you will have the ultimate peace and newness of life that will make your retirement beautiful.

Happy Birthday, Mike! Don't let this talk of retirement diminish the joy of your young life with all its zest and ambition. Instead, let your thoughts and plans for retirement give added satisfaction to these important years of your life.

> With our love,
> Uncle Sid and Aunt Lila

"Well, what do you think?" Sid asked, pushing his glasses up on his forehead.

Lila beamed at her inquiring husband. "I think we're giving Mike a gift that comes straight from our hearts, Sid. And that's the most beautiful kind of gift there is."

▪ Something to Talk About ▪

1. Describe Sid and Lila's marriage. What is their relationship like in retirement? How are they feeling about this phase of their lives? Describe other marriage relationships of retired couples you know.

2. Describe Sid and Lila's philosophy of retirement. How are they living out their philosophy?

3. Reread the letter Sid and Lila have written to Mike. Go over each of the four main points. Do you agree or disagree with them? What can you add? If you are retired, what are your reactions to their retirement ideas? If you are still working, what are your reactions?

4. What good things can happen to a marriage in retirement? What difficulties may a marriage encounter when a couple retires?

5. How can a couple prepare their marriage for retirement? How can they continue to grow in their relationship after retirement? What role might their family play?

6. What community, state, or national organizations do you know of that help retired people? How can the church be of help? What do you think the church could do to enrich the marriages of retired people? to prepare younger people for their retirement years?

8

▪ When Addiction Results ▪ in Alienation

"Where have you been?" The shrill voice and slurred words startled Tom. Margaret stood in the doorway to the garage, her hands on her hips. Her dressing gown hung loosely and unevenly around her bare feet. "I woke up and you were gone. Where have you been?"

Tom slammed the car door and fidgeted with the lock for a moment, buying time. What a surprise to find Margaret up and about. What should he tell her? Should he lie and say he'd been helping Fred with his car, or should he tell her the truth?

"Well?" Margaret stepped back to let Tom in the door. "I didn't hear you leave, but I woke about 9 P.M. and you were gone. It's almost 11 now. Where have you been?"

"Let me hang up my coat, and I'll tell you all about my evening," Tom said, closing and locking the door. He disappeared into the front hall.

Tom reappeared in the family room, where Margaret had settled on the sofa, holding a full glass of wine. Tom sat in the recliner, wondering how he was going to explain the evening. Who would have thought his wife would still be up? Most other evenings she was dead to the world by 7:30 P.M.

"I'm surprised to find you up," Tom said.

"Yeah, well, the telephone was ringing, and I got up to answer it. Clint has to work late." Margaret drank her wine.

"Oh, they must be busy at the station."

"So? You'd better confess, Tom. I've got the goods on you now. You better tell me all about your young floozy." Margaret narrowed her eyes as she stared fuzzily at her husband.

"Young floozy? What in the world—? Oh, I see," Tom said. "You think I've been out with someone. No, Margaret, I'm afraid you're all wrong. The truth is that I've been attending my first Alanon meeting."

Margaret frowned and looked confused. "Your first what?"

"Alanon meeting. I've been thinking of going for a long time, but tonight I finally got up the courage to go."

"I don't understand," Margaret said, momentarily forgetting the wine. "Alanon? What's that?"

Tom shifted in the chair. "Alanon is a special organization for the spouses and loved ones of alcoholics. I just decided I can't fight this alone anymore."

A glint of comprehension shone in Margaret's eyes. "Are you saying you went to a meeting and said I was an alcoholic?"

"Not in so many words. But, yes, my being there would imply that you or someone I love is an alcoholic." Tom watched his wife carefully. He had anticipated this moment many times in his imagination. What would she do?

Disbelief, amazement, and anger flickered across Margaret's face. "You told everyone I'm an *alcoholic*?"

"Margaret, I know *you* don't believe that, but I do. I've watched you drink yourself into oblivion, and you won't stop. I need help so I can help you."

"Damn you!" Margaret struggled up from the sofa and slammed the wine glass on the end table. Red liquid sprayed all over the furniture. "You liar! You betrayed me." She stumbled heavily about the room, threatening her husband with her fist.

Tom's heart pounded. He'd dreaded this confrontation and certainly never had expected it would come on the night of his first meeting. "Calm down, Margaret, calm down," he said in what he hoped was a soothing voice. Inside he was trembling. Margaret had hit him before in a drunken rage. He hoped she was sober enough now to contain herself. But she was very angry.

"I *live* in this town, you creep! Now *everybody* will think I'm an alcoholic! Good God, everyone knows that I have these terrible migraine headaches. My doctor knows that. He gives me lots of medicine for them. Sure, I take a drink once in a while but I'm *not* an alcoholic! How could you do this to me? You're the one who makes me drink." Margaret continued to rant as she walked erratically about the room. Suddenly she took a swing at a table lamp, knocking it to the floor and shattering it. Sparks flew. Tom hurried to the wall socket and jerked the plug out.

"Stop it, you crazy woman!" Tom yelled. "You're drunk, and you're going to destroy this house." He grabbed Margaret and pushed her down on the sofa. "Sit there and shut up! *I'm* going to talk." Breathing hard in his exertion and anger, Tom stood over Margaret. Her lower lip was quivering. All the fight had gone out of her. "I don't know how much you're going to understand tonight, but I'm going to say it anyway. I am *not* the reason you drink too much. And Clint and Jason aren't the reasons either. You are a sick, sick woman, and you *are* an alcoholic. This booze controls your life." Tom shook his finger at Margaret who watched him in blurry puzzlement. "First it started with those cocktail parties in the neighborhood. Then it grew into keeping—even hiding—wine and Scotch in the house. Then it was a matter of finding you so stewed you couldn't fix dinner or clean the house. Sure, you've told everyone you have migraine headaches and that's why you're sick and keep the house so dark. Do you honestly think anyone believes you? Good grief, it was your doctor who told me to go to Alanon. He wants you to go to Alcoholics Anonymous." Tom was running out of steam. He looked wearily around the room, then began picking up the broken lamp.

Margaret frowned and tipped over sideways on the sofa. Her head hit the end table with a sharp crack. "Ow!" she moaned. "Don't hit me!"

"Don't be stupid!" Tom shouted from the other side of the room. "I'm way over here. How could I hit you? You're so drunk you don't even know you banged your own head on the table."

Margaret wept and pushed herself upright. "I don't like it when you yell at me, Tommy. How come you don't love me anymore? How come you don't hug and kiss me?"

Tom swept the pieces of glass into the dust pan and dumped them in the basket. He left the twisted lamp shade on the kitchen counter. Sitting in the recliner again, Tom sighed and rubbed his eyes. "You've got it all wrong, Margaret. I *do* love you. Only God knows why. I couldn't have stuck it out this long if I didn't care so much. But it's no fun to hug and kiss you anymore, because you look and act like such a drunken tramp, and you smell like a barroom floor. Being in bed with you means listening to a freight train all night. It's easier to sleep in Jason's old room. At least I can rest in there."

Margaret looked forlornly at her husband. "You hate me."

"No, of course I don't hate you. Why do you keep saying that? Don't you realize that I could have left you years ago, but I've chosen to stay? You're the one who pushes *me* away." Tom laid his head back, closing his eyes. "You were so beautiful. I can remember—on our wedding day you wore that white lace dress your mother made, and your black hair just cascaded down your back. You wore a crown of flowers, and some of the petals were caught in your long hair. I thought you were an absolute vision. And I remember our first little house, Maggie. Both Jason and Clint were born there, and you were so loving and so caring and so much fun. I thought I was the luckiest man in the world."

Tom glanced at Margaret. She was lying on the sofa, watching him. "I wonder where Clint is?" she said vaguely.

"He's working late, don't you remember?"

"Well, where's Jason?"

Tom looked away in disgust and pain. "Jason lives in Albany now, Margaret. He's lived there two years."

"Jason hates me, too."

"Well, if he does, you made him do it. That's all I can say." Tom's voice was bitter. He stared at the dark TV screen. "I don't know how many times you've embarrassed those boys in front of their friends. I wish I'd known about the group for teenagers when Jason was still home. I'm going to talk to Clint about joining it, even though he's out of high school. If Alateen can do for him what I think Alanon can do for me—"

"What did you do at your meeting?" Margaret's eyes were closed now.

"Well, I mainly listened tonight. I was fascinated to hear other people talk about the same things I've been experiencing: the anger, the disgust, the fear, the alienation, the loneliness. I thought I was the only one in the world who felt that way, but here's a whole bunch of people who understand what it means to have someone you love be an alcoholic and to feel so helpless as you watch that person destroy himself or herself, and feel as if you're being destroyed too. I didn't say much tonight, just asked a few questions. But next week or the week after that I'll talk too. It'll feel so good just to talk."

A loud snore erupted from Margaret. Her arm hung over the side of the sofa. Her hair straggled across her face.

Tom watched his wife as she slept in her usual drunken stupor. "Oh, Margaret," he whispered. "I wish you could be Maggie again."

• Something to Talk About •

1. Why does addiction (to drugs, alcohol, gambling, etc.) result in alienation from the people in one's family, neighborhood, and acquaintances?

2. Alcoholism is an illness. Tell what you know about it. Why can some people drink alcohol moderately, but others, like Margaret, become victims of addiction?

3. Describe the marriage relationship Tom and Margaret have now. How do you think Margaret may be feeling? How does Tom feel? Is there any hope for this marriage?

4. What do you think can or should be done about this situation? What will Tom be learning and gaining at the Alanon meetings? If you are familiar with this organization, describe it. How could Alateen help Clint? When will Margaret be able to join Alcoholics Anonymous? What other sources of help may be available?

5. If you've had any experience with a marriage like this, describe it. Also describe what was done to help the situation and how it turned out.

6. What local community resources are available to you to help addicted people and their loved ones?

7. What role can the church play in helping the addicted person and the families involved? Why are church members often quick to criticize and even condemn people caught in this trap?

9

▪ When Former Marriages ▪ Are a Factor

Sitting at her desk, Maryann heard a strange noise in the backyard. No one was home except herself. Who was inside the fence? Leaving her typewriter and manuscript, Maryann quietly walked to the sliding glass door and peered outside. Seeing a movement, she quickly opened the door and grabbed a croquet mallet, trying to get a better look. Suddenly Chuck came around the corner of the garage.

"What in the world?" he gasped, seeing his wife with the upraised mallet.

Maryann let out a huge sigh of relief, as she lowered her weapon. "It's you! Oh, I'm so glad it's you! What are you doing home at this hour? It's not even two o'clock!"

Chuck laughed as he locked the side gate. "Can't a guy check on his garden without being attacked? The weeds are taking over out here."

They walked together into the house. "I *am* glad to see you, but you gave me a scare, Chuck! Good heavens! I thought a burglar was trying to get in."

"How about a cup of coffee for the burglar?" Chuck gave Maryann a quick hug. "And how about having a cup with me?"

Maryann poured two cups of coffee, then cut a piece of pie for her husband. "Here you go, burglar. Eat and enjoy." Maryann sat down at the kitchen table with Chuck. "You still haven't told me why you're home at two in the afternoon."

Chuck sipped the hot coffee and cut off the tip of the pie wedge with his fork. "Mmmmm, good!" he said, tasting the tangy apples. After finishing the pie he drank his coffee. "Well, I'm afraid I have some bad news, Maryann. I decided I should tell you right away. I couldn't have worked at the shop any longer anyway."

"Now you're scaring me again," Maryann said, her eyes wide with fear. "Is it Jim? Or Ellen? What's wrong?"

Chuck pulled a folded letter from his pocket. "This came to the shop at noon. It's for you."

Maryann slowly took the letter from Chuck. "It's open," she said faintly.

"When I saw who it was from, I had to see what he wanted. Sorry." Chuck finished his coffee, not looking at his wife.

"It's from Les. I can't believe it. I haven't heard from him in—well, it's got to be five years or more. Since his mother died." Maryann gingerly pulled the letter from the envelope and began to read silently.

Chuck rummaged in his pockets and found his pipe. Lighting it, he watched his wife from the corner of his eye. The tears were pouring down her face as she read the letter. He looked away, puffing on the pipe.

Maryann finished reading and slowly folded the letter, sliding it back into the envelope. "I can't believe it. I just can't believe it."

"I know," Chuck said. "I felt the same way. I'm sorry I opened it. Even after all these years, I felt the jealousy wash right over me, and I had to see what Les was telling you. I really felt like a creep when I read it."

Maryann stood up and put her arms out to Chuck. She cried and cried as he embraced her and tried to comfort her. "I'm sorry. I'm so sorry," he said over and over.

Finally, after blowing her nose and wiping the tears away, Maryann was able to speak. "Who would have thought my ex-husband would write a letter like that? He's been so angry these past 12 years. Now, as he's dying in that hospital, he writes that beautiful letter. He forgives me—and you, too, Chuck. After all these years, after all these feelings." The tears started flowing again. Chuck put his arm around her shoulders and led Maryann into the living room. They sat together on the sofa.

"I can't believe it. I can't believe it," Maryann whispered, fingering the letter. "He's got cancer of the pancreas. The doctor says he probably won't live six months. He's trying to get his life in order, he says."

"He loved you a lot," Chuck said. "That was what made it so hard. If he'd been mean to you or beaten you or just didn't care, but he loved you. And I've always been afraid—"

"Of what?" Maryann asked quickly.

"Afraid you might go back to him."

"Oh, no! I'd *never* do that! Ever since we met, I've known you were the only man for me," Maryann protested. "It's just that it was so difficult—all of us working in the shop the way we did. We knew each other so well, and I've always carried so much guilt about what we did to Les. Then when he tried to commit suicide—"

"That's over, and he did it just to scare us anyway. Now my wife—there was a *real* case for you. I never felt guilty about her." Chuck's face was grim.

"But I know you've felt badly about the boys. You said many times that if you'd been able to be a real father to them, they probably wouldn't have gotten so mixed up."

Chuck got up from the sofa to pace and relight his pipe. "What a mess we made for ourselves! Sometimes I've wondered—"

"Be careful," Maryann warned. "Wondering is dangerous for a marriage. Especially one that has as many strikes against it as ours."

"And what about the guilt you've felt?" Chuck said sharply. "Isn't that dangerous to the health of a marriage?"

Maryann dropped her eyes and stared at the letter in her lap. "I just can't help it, Chuck. I know, God has forgiven me for all the mistakes I've made, including the adultery. But I haven't been able to forgive myself. The wreckage is all around us. We broke up two families because we fell in love and insisted on having each other. And what happens? My ex-husband is hurt terribly and tries to kill himself. Your ex-wife lives on tranquilizers, and the kids run wild. Neither of them marries again, and both of them are miserable. And now this! Les is dying, and he's all alone. His mother is dead, his brother is dead, no children to care for him. Just me. Can you believe it? I'm the one who hurt him the most, and he writes to *me!*" Maryann's tears spilled on the rumpled letter, making the ink run.

Chuck gazed out the sliding glass door, into the garden. "It's ironic, that's for sure."

Long moments passed as Maryann sobbed and sniffed on the sofa. Chuck stared at the garden. The weeds were so tall he could barely see the flowers. Here and there he saw a pink or yellow blossom. He really had to get out there and take charge of things. "We've had a good marriage. Don't you dare forget that."

"Yes, I know. It's amazed me sometimes, but we're good for each other. We can talk and laugh. We work well together."

"And look at the good things we've accomplished. Our work at church is so exciting! And we've even been asked to write that material for organizing couples' groups in the national church. We can really be proud and happy about what we've done together. I see that you've been working on it," Chuck said, looking at her desk.

"Yes, I'm on the second section now." Maryann stood up and went to the desk, placing the letter carefully in the mail rack. "And things are getting better with your kids. Now that they're in their 20s you've at least been able to talk to them."

"That's *really* something to be happy about! They call once in a while, and I think they're beginning to understand me better. I know I'm getting to know them." Chuck smiled a little. "That should make you feel good, Maryann. I know you've felt just as badly about the boys as I have."

"But I still carry the guilt about Les. And now this!" Maryann folded her arms tightly in front of her, staring at the floor. "Sometimes I think God is punishing me. We've never been able to have children, and we wanted them so much. We've lived with one eye fixed on the door and one ear open for the phone, never knowing if our ex-spouses would be doing something to hurt us."

"Look, Maryann. Les said he forgives us both. That should end it for you."

"Then why do I feel so terrible?" Maryann demanded. "God must be punishing me."

"Stop it!" Chuck's voice was firm. "You know better than that. God doesn't go around wreaking vengeance on his children. What we're experiencing here is the natural consequences of our deeds. See those weeds out there?" Chuck said, pointing to the garden. "I think you've got to pull your weeds of guilt and misery so you can see the bright and beautiful flower of our marriage. It's not enough just to be sorry. God forgives, but I believe it's up to us to do what we can to mend relationships between ourselves."

"Me? Mend the relationship with Les?" Maryann looked at Chuck and then gazed at the letter in the mail file. "Well, he said he's in St. John's Hospital in Tacoma. Maybe I should go to see him."

"Maybe *we* should go to see him," Chuck said.

▪ Something to Talk About ▪

1. Describe Chuck and Maryann's marriage. What's good about it? What has been difficult? What feelings does Maryann have? How does Chuck feel?

2. What pressures have been placed on this marriage right from the start? What sort of resolutions are gradually taking place that are relieving some of the pressure?

3. Using Chuck's analogy of the flowers and weeds in his garden, discuss what has happened to this marriage and what needs to be done to allow it to grow and develop. What does Chuck mean when he says, "What we're experiencing here is the natural consequences of our deeds"? How would you suggest this couple try to relieve the guilt Maryann continues to feel? How does James 1:19-25 apply to this situation?

4. Every marriage has unique pressures, joys, and problems. If you are familiar with the course a second or third marriage has taken, describe the ways the couple has coped with its special circumstances. Who or what was of particular help?

5. Children of former marriages, especially when they live with the new couple, often present special situations and pressures for a marriage. Describe how these pressures can be coped with for the benefit of everyone involved.

6. What community resources are available for people formerly married and now in new marriages? for parents and stepparents? What message does the church have that can help, comfort, and strengthen people such as Maryann and Chuck? In what other ways can the church be of help?

10

▪ When a Couple's Child ▪ Dies

Roy stowed the cooking gear in the cupboards beneath the bed. The tent trailer was filled with cubbyholes, and Carolyn had neatly labeled each door with the names of the items that belonged in that space.

Outside, Carolyn sat on the picnic table bench, staring at the Texas sunset. She sipped her second cup of coffee. It had been a long ride from the Gulf.

"Do you want a cookie to go with the coffee, Carolyn?" Roy asked, poking his head out the trailer door. He waved the bag of fig newtons in his wife's direction.

"No, thanks anyway," Carolyn said, still staring at the horizon. "All this riding and sitting means I can't burn off the calories."

Roy closed the trailer door and joined Carolyn on the bench. "You're so strong-willed when it comes to a diet. It's a good thing fig newtons aren't my favorite cookie or I'd be devouring the whole package. I get so hungry when we're outdoors like this."

"There's going to be plenty to eat at the family reunion, Roy. You know how grandma and all the aunts and uncles like to cook."

Roy smiled dreamily at the thought. "Wasn't it five years ago that Harry and Ruth roasted the pig? The reunion was in Iowa that year, I remember. And Marcy ate all those juicy pork ribs."

Carolyn stood up suddenly and became busy with the coffeepot on the fireplace grill. She poured another few inches of coffee into her cup. Her hands were shaking so that the stream of liquid wobbled.

"For crying out loud, Carolyn! Can't I even say our daughter's name?" Roy asked in disgust. "It's unnatural not to talk about our only child."

Carolyn put the coffeepot down on the grill and held her cup with both hands, gently blowing the steam away from her face. "It hurts to talk about her, Roy. I'm sorry."

Roy got up to embrace his wife from the back, carefully avoiding the hot cup of coffee. He kissed the side of her face, smelling the fragrance of her hair. "I know it hurts, darling, but it's as Pastor Roberts said, we've got to break down this wall between us. He said talking and openness and honesty are the only things that are going to do it." Carolyn stood rigidly in his embrace, continuing to stare at the sunset and blow on the coffee.

"OK," Roy said, abruptly releasing her and going to sit on the picnic table, his feet on the bench. "If you won't talk, then I will. I have to. These four months since Marcy was killed have been agony for me, just as I know they have been for you."

Carolyn whirled around and spoke through clenched teeth. "Don't, Roy, please don't. I'm held together by a thread, a very thin one. I don't want to lose control of myself, certainly not out here in the Texas wilds."

"I can't think of a better place to do it, sweetheart. There's no one around for miles. Only God himself is listening to us. It's time, Carolyn. We have to lay our daughter to rest and pull our lives together."

"Things will never, ever be good again, Roy!" Carolyn said fiercely. "Marcy is gone, I'm completely empty—and what's worse, I know I killed her."

"You didn't kill her! You happened to be driving the car when that drunk driver sped through the stoplight. There wasn't anything you could have done about it. Every policeman and every witness to the accident said the same thing. It was a miracle *you* lived through it," Roy protested.

"I wish I'd died instead of her," Carolyn said, choking on the words, "or that I'd died with her. I can't take this pain. And you're making it worse." She was facing the horizon again. The orange sunset was fading.

"I know you feel that way. Part of me feels like that too. But the fact is that you and I are alive. We have to make our lives count, Carolyn. We can't exist in this bitterness and pain. With God's help we have to refocus our lives. We need goals, things to look forward to and to work for, just as the pastor said."

Carolyn put her cup down on the trailer step and faced Roy, her hands on her hips. "All right. You want honesty and openness? I'll give you honesty and openness." She paused, staring at Roy, her lips pursed and her eyes narrowed. "I blame myself for Marcy's death, because I feel that somehow I should have seen that car coming and somehow I should have gotten out of the way. But you want to know something? I really and truly blame *you* even more!"

Roy swallowed hard. He felt numb. The dam was about to break. He forced himself to be quiet.

"That's right—I blame *you* for Marcy's death. It's your fault. I wouldn't have had to drive Marcy to Mrs. Allen's house that afternoon if *you* hadn't insisted that her piano lesson be changed. And *why* did you want it changed?" Carolyn asked sarcastically, leaning toward her husband. "Because *you* wanted to play golf Saturday morning, and Marcy's lesson would interfere. Here's a big news flash for you: my beautiful 10-year-old girl is lying cold in the ground because her father loved golf more than his daughter. How's *that* for honesty and openness, hot shot?" Carolyn picked up the coffee cup and hurled it into the scrub brush. She swung her other arm at the coffeepot on the grill, knocking it six feet away against the tent trailer. Brown stains spread on the canvas. For a moment Carolyn stared in surprise and alarm. Then she ran around the trailer and into the small grove of trees.

Roy's heart was pounding wildly. He could hardly catch his breath. Dear God, what was he going to do? Should he go get her, or wait until she returned? Should he tell her his honest feelings, or let the whole thing rest?

Ten long minutes passed. Roy sat like a statue on the picnic table. Then he heard slow footsteps behind him. "Carolyn? Is that you?"

"Yes, it's me," her quiet voice said. "Don't worry, no monster is coming to get you." Carolyn carefully seated herself on the table beside her husband. "OK, I'm ready now."

Roy looked at her, frowning. "Ready for what?" Tear stains were all over her face, and her mascara had left brown smudges under her eyes.

"Ready for you to be honest with me. I told you what I thought. Now it's your turn."

Roy blew a deep breath through his lips, puffing his cheeks momentarily. "Wow!" Another blowing breath escaped. "Well, I blame myself for just the reasons you said. I can't believe I wanted to play golf and that resulted in Marcy's death." Carolyn tried to say something, but Roy stopped her. "Let me talk this out, now that I've started. I'm going to cry, but I've got to get it out. Carolyn, I blame myself but—I've got to say this—I blame *you*, too. Not for the actual accident, because nobody could have done anything about that. But it's your fault that I insisted on playing golf that Saturday. Remember how you told everyone at that party that I was no good at golf, that for me a par score was always six above the average? I never told you, Carolyn, but that really hurt. I know it's stupid, but I pride myself on my golf game. My dad taught me to play, and you know what a great golfer he was, winning tournaments and all. That Saturday golf game I was going to play in was the Country Club Classic Tournament. I was partnered with the pro from the club, and I knew I had a great chance of winning it all. I wanted to show you and our friends that I was a good golfer." Roy was sobbing the words out. Tears spilled everywhere and his nose was running. "If you hadn't humiliated me in front of our friends, I wouldn't have wanted to get back at you, and I wouldn't have insisted on playing that Saturday. Dear God in heaven, I blame you just as much as I blame myself!" Roy finally buried his face in his arms, leaning forward on his knees. Loud sobs and groans poured out.

Carolyn was sobbing, too, as she pulled him into her arms. "I'm sorry, I'm sorry," they both cried, soaking each other's hair and jackets. "I love you, I love you." Night birds and insects chattered. The new moon glowed in the dark sky.

When they finally released each other, they were smiling and laughing a little. "Gosh, this is wet," Roy said. "I never realized how much water came out of eyes."

"Perhaps we need to think of it like a baptism," Carolyn said, wiping her face.

The thought stopped Roy in his tracks. "That's right. A baptism. The Lord has given us a new start in the Texas wilderness. He's baptized us into a new life with our own tears. That's really beautiful!"

Carolyn picked up the fallen coffeepot and found her cup in the brush. Fanning the coals in the fireplace, she revived the flames. "Well, the coffee is gone, but I can make more if you want it."

"No, don't bother," Roy said. "Come here and sit with me. We'll just enjoy looking at the fire. That's very symbolic too. John the Baptist said that Christ would baptize with the Holy Spirit and with fire."

Carolyn laughed. "I can't believe how much better I feel. I said all those ugly things and you said all those ugly things— and we fall in each other's arms. How does that work anyway?"

"I guess we really love each other. Perhaps we had to get the infection out before the healing could start. It's going to be better now, sweetheart. Marcy will always be a part of us, and we're going to love her and miss her, but—"

"But I think now we can begin to belong to each other again, Roy."

• Something to Talk About •

1. Briefly tell the story of Marcy's death. Name at least three strong feelings Carolyn and Roy have been experiencing. Why do you think they haven't expressed the anger and blame before?

2. Pastor Roberts had counseled them to try to break down the wall between them. What was this wall? What had created it? What finally broke the wall down? What difference do you think the isolated location made?

3. Why does communication—even angry communication—open doors and break down walls? What does this say about daily, ordinary communication in marriage?

4. It's easy to glibly say, "Marcy is with Jesus," but what words of hope and comfort from the Scriptures and Christian experience will speak to Roy and Carolyn?

5. Roy and Carolyn see themselves at the beginning of a new life. Does this mean they'll never grieve for Marcy again? that they'll never disagree about her death and the reasons for it? that everything will be wonderful from now on? What do you think a couple's "new life" can be like after their child has died?

6. If you have lost a child (to death, drugs, running away, etc.) or know someone who has, describe the feelings a parent has at this time. What things helped you or your friends? Why are some families broken by separation and divorce following the loss of a child? Why are other families drawn closer together?

7. How can the church minister to a couple who has lost a child in death? Why are groups of parents who have all lost children an important counseling and therapy experience? What helps for bereaved parents are available in your church and/or community?

11

▪ When an Older Parent ▪
Lives with a Couple

The news commentator was explaining the American and Russian summit talks when Janet slowly entered the house. It had been a very long day at Redmond Industries, and her new executive position demanded much from her mentally and emotionally. It was good to be home.

By the cooking aroma Janet knew Bob had prepared the roast chicken after all. Of course, it was his mother's favorite dish. No matter that Janet was sick to death of chicken. Anything mother wanted, mother got. *Now be careful,* Janet reminded herself. *The last thing you need tonight is a knock-down-drag-out fight about Lydia and her influence on her only son.*

"Finally got home, I see," Bob's grin made the remark less stinging than it could have been. "I saved your dinner in the microwave. Just have to heat it up again. I'm watching the news with mother in her room. She wasn't feeling too good, so we both ate in there. There's a feature coming on about word processors that I want to see. Why don't you bring your plate in there and keep us company?"

"No, I think I'll just stay out here in the kitchen," Janet demurred. "I'll read the paper, and then I'll clean up the dishes." Bob had already left to see his news feature.

By 8 P.M. Janet was deep in her correspondence. A week's worth of letters had piled up on her desk, so she had taken them home to read. Bob was busy at his typewriter in the den. Janet momentarily wondered how he managed to write his magazine articles and keep up on the housework too. Everything had gotten so hectic ever since his mother moved in six months ago.

Soon Janet's attention was back on her letters.

By 10 P.M. Bob was watching a mystery drama with his mother in her room. Janet was soaking in a bubble bath.

By 11 P.M. Bob and Janet were preparing for bed. "Bob, my boss is planning an important dinner at the Century Club next Friday night, and he's invited us both to come. Can I tell him tomorrow that we'll be there?"

"Friday? Well, I don't know. Mother has a dental appointment in the afternoon. She'll probably be pretty uncomfortable by evening. Maybe we should plan to be home with her."

"Bob, your mother is capable of taking care of herself for a while. A few hours in the evening shouldn't be a problem. Let me talk to her." Janet made a move toward the door.

"No, no, don't do that." Bob almost blocked her way. "I don't want to upset her. She's had a hard day."

"*She's* had a hard day! What about *me*? You didn't even ask what *my* day was like! Honestly, Bob, you baby her too much. We don't have any life of our own anymore. If I'd known things would be like this, I never would have agreed to have her live with us."

"You would have sent her to a nursing home, I suppose?" Bob demanded. "And what makes you think this is an easy situation for me? I'm supposed to be a writer, but it's hard to be creative when I'm answering her bell all the time."

Janet stared at Bob, then dropped to the edge of the bed. "Bob, that's the first time I've ever heard you complain about the situation. I thought you really liked it this way. *I'm* the one who feels so left out and lonesome."

Bob snorted, turning the covers down on the bed. "I'm doing what I think I should do. I feel responsible for mother now that dad's gone. But that doesn't make it easy. Don't you think I want things the way they were before? One of the reasons I liked working at home was that I could fit my schedule to yours. We used to do a lot of great things, and we had time to talk and laugh. The way it is now, I hardly get to see you alone. The bedroom is the only place we really have to ourselves anymore."

"Come on," Janet said softly, crawling into bed beside Bob. "Turn off the light, and let's be real friendly again."

When Janet turned toward Bob, the bed squeaked. It squeaked loudly again when Bob turned off the light. Once again it creaked and squeaked when Janet adjusted her pillow and tried to get comfortable.

"Shhhh," Bob warned. "Mother is right beneath us in her room, and I know she's not asleep yet."

"What difference does that make? This is our bedroom! We're alone here. You just got through saying this was the only place—"

"I know, I know," Bob whispered. "But I noticed the other day when you were up here resting and I was in mother's room, that the squeaky bed can be heard very plainly down there."

"And you don't want her knowing that we're making love?" Janet asked incredulously.

"Well, it bothers me to know she can hear every move. It's almost like a play-by-play description. Doesn't that bother you?"

Janet sighed. "Yes, I have to admit it does. We've got to get this bed oiled."

"I've tried, Janet, but I can't find the squeaky parts. It's hard to oil a place and then jump on the bed to find out if it worked."

Suddenly Janet started to giggle. And once started, she couldn't stop. The very idea of Bob trying to oil the bed, then jumping on it! The giggles turned into gales of laughter, which she tried to muffle in her pillow. Soon Bob was laughing, too, big tears pouring down his face. And through it all, the bed squeaked and creaked.

"Mother must think we're really having a terrific time up here!" Janet managed to say between giggles.

Half an hour later, exhausted from laughing and lovemaking, Bob and Janet sat in the comfortable armchairs by the window in their bedroom.

"That's exactly what I miss the most, Janet—being with you and having the kind of fun we had before—"

"I know—before your mother came here to live. I miss it, too, Bob. And we hardly have any time to talk about things anymore. I miss our talks so much." Janet was reapplying cold cream to her face.

"I think I've finally figured something out, though. With mother in the house and being with her so much, I feel as if I'm her little boy again, Janet. I'm 45 years old, and for the past six months I've felt 10 years old again. If she says to do something, I run and do it. If she complains about something, I have to fix it. If she looks sad, I feel responsible."

"Bob, that's called *manipulation*. Excuse me if I sound harsh, but I'm sure she knows exactly what she's doing to you, and she's playing it for all it's worth."

"Well, I don't know about that," Bob said. "But I sure wish I could take charge of my own life again."

"You *can*. *We* can!"

"I won't send her to a nursing home, Janet. Difficult as this is, at least I'm not racked with guilt. I'll never forget how my dad worried about mother being in a home."

"Of course not, silly. Anyone can see your mother doesn't belong in a nursing home. She's too active and too sharp. And, Bob, she's not nearly as sick as she'd have you believe. Dr. Fellows made that very plain."

"I know, I heard him say it, too. But what can we do? She expects a lot of attention."

Janet stifled a huge yawn. "One thing we never did when your mother came here was to establish some ground rules. It's really like having a teenager in the house, Bob. Even though our kids are both grown and gone, we've got to establish some rules that we expect mother to follow, just as we did with the kids."

"Rules? For my mother?" Bob sounded dumbfounded.

"Yes, and don't make me start laughing again! She has to know that we expect to live our own lives. And, Bob, there are a lot of things she can do around the house to help out. Older people need to feel needed. I read that someplace the other day. Think of how much more time you'd have for writing if mother were doing something constructive instead of having you wait on her."

"Maybe you're right. She's always asking me about my writing. Maybe I could involve her in the process somehow."

"Another thing, Bob. I heard Pastor Sands talking about a counseling service that has to do with aging. Maybe they could help us with some ideas and resources." Janet yawned again until her jaw cracked.

"Come on, sweet thing, you've got to sleep." Bob pulled Janet out of her chair and into bed. "We can talk about this in the morning. And tell your boss we'll go to the dinner. I'll figure something out for mother on Friday night."

As Bob crawled into bed and turned out the light, the bed squeaked loudly.

▪ Something to Talk About ▪

1. Describe the situation in Bob and Janet's home. How is each of them feeling about it?

2. What is happening to their marriage? to their communication? What has happened to their priorities? In particular, what has happened to Bob's feelings, attitudes, and behavior?

3. Have you had the experience of an older parent living in your home? What special pressures or problems did it bring? What joys and satisfactions did it offer? How did you organize your household so as to bring comfort to all parties?

4. Note the role reversal in Bob and Janet's marriage. Are they comfortable with that? What new role reversal is called for between Bob and his mother?

5. What advice could you give to Bob and Janet as they work to reorganize their lives with his mother in the home? What role might the church play in this situation? What community resources are available?

12

▪ When a Couple Copes ▪ with Unemployment

"Ken, are you awake?"

"Yup."

"I have an idea."

"What?"

"Why don't you get up and turn on the lights?"

There was silence from the other side of the hideaway bed.

"Ken? Are you awake?" Evelyn peered at the dark hump that was her husband. It wasn't moving.

"I'm awake, but I'm trying to remember where the light switch is."

Evelyn started to giggle. "That's what you get for making me sleep next to the wall! Maybe we're stuck here until the sun comes up."

"Why do you want the lights on anyway? Just tell me your idea."

The giggling continued. "Actually I didn't mean the light switch. I was thinking—since we're both wide awake anyway, we could turn on the Christmas tree lights. How many times do we get to lie in bed and look at a Christmas tree?"

The dark hump shifted in the bed and faced the ceiling.

"And how do you propose that I find the cord for the Christmas tree, not to mention the wall outlet to plug the cord into?"

Evelyn was trying to suppress the giggles in her pillow. "Shhh, Andrea and Neil are just on the other side of this wall. They'll hear us," Evelyn said.

Ken sat on the edge of the pull-out bed. The metal brace dug into his thighs. "OK, here goes." He began crawling on the floor toward the shadow of the Christmas tree. Evelyn sat up in bed, watching the progress of the dark hump. She had the covers jammed in her mouth to keep from laughing too loudly. "Found the branches . . . found the presents . . . found some bulbs . . . aha! Found the cord." Evelyn could see the shadowy tree sway slightly. Suddenly the Christmas tree came to life. Ken's pajama bottoms were facing Evelyn as he squirmed backward, out from under the tree. Evelyn collapsed on the bed in helpless laughter. Ken crawled back in beside her and started to laugh, too. He put his arms around Evelyn, and they laughed together as the Christmas lights merrily blinked on and off in a rainbow pattern across the bed. When they had worn themselves out laughing, they lay back to look at the tree. The paper ornaments the grandchildren had made were slowly turning. The stars softly glowed over the manger scene.

"Isn't that pretty, Ken? I wanted to see the tree one more time on Christmas Eve." Evelyn kept her voice to a low whisper.

"It's real nice. It was a real nice party tonight too." Ken folded his arms behind his head as he watched the lights go on and off. "I'm glad we made the trip, Evelyn. I was thinking we really shouldn't spend the money on the gas, but if we didn't drive then we'd have to mail the presents."

"Oh, we had to come to Andrea's for Christmas." Evelyn shifted in the bed. The metal crossbar was hitting her tailbone the wrong way. "And we had to see the youngsters' faces when they opened the presents you made for them. Julie loved her dollhouse. Did you see her eyes light up?"

"I sure did." Ken was smiling. "And I got such a kick out of Troy as he ran around here with that alligator pull toy. I'm so glad I thought to put the jingle bells on it."

Evelyn turned to face her husband. The colored lights were dancing. "It was so nice I forgot about our troubles for a while, honey. And just think—we can stay here until New Year's. I don't have to be back to work until Tuesday."

Ken gently touched Evelyn's feet with his toes. "I know, and I'm so glad. You've worked such long hours in that school kitchen, and you really deserve a break." He sighed deeply. His mouth set into his habitual expression of sadness. "Dear God, I feel so worthless sometimes."

"Oh, Ken, I wish you wouldn't feel that way—especially at Christmas. We've got so much to be thankful for, and it's such a treat to be here at Andrea's."

"I know, but the whole thing just haunts me. I can't believe it. Thirty years at the plant right down the tubes. The union is busted, most of my pension benefits are gone, my job is all washed up. Some other yo-yo is welding body parts together, and here I am—55 years old and looking for work. It's been almost a year since we voted to strike."

Evelyn sighed and laid her arm across Ken's chest. "But you've been trying so hard to find something else, honey, and you've had some temporary jobs. One of these days the right thing will turn up."

Ken ground his teeth and made disgusted noises. "We've been saying that for a year. I've been to the job counseling center. I've been evaluated three times for other kinds of work. The unemployment checks have stopped. I can't even provide *that* for you anymore. You have to work in that old kitchen. What's going to become of us?" The tears rolled down Ken's face.

"The Lord has provided for us, Ken," Evelyn said. "I'm just

so glad I've got that job at Perpetual Help School. Think of the food they've given me to take home. I wouldn't have had any of that if I worked at a store or at the hospital."

"I know all that, and I know God has provided. I don't mean to sound ungrateful, but, Evelyn, do you have any idea how important a man's work is to him? I never realized it myself until I was without my job. Now I know that my work made me feel I was worth something. I felt like I was somebody. I had a schedule to follow. That's one of the hardest things, strangely enough. I miss having a set schedule."

Evelyn laughed a little. "As I remember, you used to gripe about that schedule."

"I know I did. Now I wish I had it back. It all makes me so mad! Who would have thought the company could outlast the union? Talk about making a wrong choice! If only I hadn't agreed to strike.

"Life is filled with 'if onlys,' Ken. We've got to hang on and look forward." Evelyn patted her husband's face. "Right now, we really need to relax and enjoy our days here with the kids and the grandchildren. They sure loved the toys you made for them."

"Doesn't it make *you* mad, Evelyn? I'm the one who's always talking about unemployment. You never say anything except 'It's going to be OK.' Don't you have any feelings about it at all? Do you know what it's like to live with a saint without feelings?"

Evelyn drew back from Ken. She frowned as she looked at his angry face. "What do you mean, no feelings? I have plenty of feelings!"

"Yeah?" Ken said, glancing at his wife. "I think you and Pollyanna are related."

"Well, maybe we are at that. I do try to find the good in things. But that doesn't mean I don't have feelings." Evelyn sat up in bed and leaned against the sofa back. "I just thought I should spare you. I have talked to the pastor a little bit. I had a bad time about a month ago. We were so low on food, and my paycheck was a week away. That evening I went outside to find the dog and just stood there, looking at the stars. I was crying pretty hard, and I just told God."

"Told God what?" Ken whispered.

"I said, 'God, I know you haven't deserted me, but I *feel* so forsaken. I just can't help it. I feel so alone.' And then I asked the Lord for a sign, so I could know he was there and cared about me."

"And was there a sign?" Ken was fascinated by his wife's words.

"Not right that minute. But the next day I was going through my summer clothes to find a jacket I needed when I found the money." Evelyn smiled and hugged the blankets close to her.

"Money? What money?"

"Don't you remember? I told you how I found that 10-dollar bill in the pocket of my summer jacket. I'd forgotten all about it. It was the sign I needed from the Lord. We lived for a week on the food I bought with that money."

Ken gazed at his wife in amazement. "I've never heard you talk like that. I thought you weren't feeling anything."

They stared at the Christmas tree. The angel at the top stared back.

"Andrea said something interesting tonight," Ken said, his words slurring with oncoming sleep. "She was so taken with the gifts I made for the kids. She said she was sure I could sell toys like that."

"No kidding!" Evelyn sat upright. "What a great idea! Your toys are just as good as anything I've seen at those craft fairs at the shopping mall—better, in fact."

Ken's eyes were closed. "Yeah? Let's think about it tomorrow, honey. It's been a great Christmas after all."

Evelyn slid back under the covers. "It's been wonderful. I've loved it."

The lights continued to dance over their faces and on the wall behind them.

"Ken, are you still awake?"

"Mmmmmmm."

"Who's going to turn out the lights?"

▪ Something to Talk About ▪

1. Describe Ken's unemployment situation. How is he feeling about it? Be specific: try to name at least six different feelings he's experienced.

2. Now describe Evelyn's situation and her feelings. What do you think she's been doing to make Ken say, "Don't you have any feelings about it at all? Do you know what it's like to live with a saint without feelings?" How would you characterize communication in this marriage? Why is it important for Evelyn to be honest with Ken about her feelings?

3. Name some things Ken has been doing about his unemployment. What other things can you suggest that he should try? For Ken work means a paycheck, but what other things has he discovered that work means for him?

4. What sort of relationship does this couple have? Why was it important for them to take the Christmas trip? What importance does laughter play in their relationship?

5. Unemployment of the major breadwinner can cause many kinds of stress in a home, and there will be many different reactions. Name other reactions in addition to the ones depicted in this story. What can happen to marriages in the face of unemployment?

6. What help and resources are available in your community for the unemployed? What can the church do to help individuals and families experiencing unemployment? Money and bags of food are helpful, but what can the church do to help people feel better about themselves and find gainful employment?

13

▪ When Childbearing ▪
Involves a Choice

"Were you really surprised?" Mark began picking up coffee cups and dessert plates in the living room as soon as the last guest disappeared. "Tell me the truth, Bev. Didn't you suspect a party was coming tonight?"

"No, I really didn't! I'd had such a busy day at the college that I forgot it was my birthday, and when I came in the front door, I was thinking only about getting a quick dinner together. I couldn't believe it when Kathy and Mary and Bob and everybody yelled 'Surprise! You're 30 years old!' " Bev hugged herself, reliving the memory. "I don't even mind being 30 after this great party. Thanks, Mark. I know you must have set it all up."

"Kathy helped me. So did Mike." Balancing the plates and cups, Mark brought them into the kitchen. Bev followed.

"I was so glad to see Carol and Stan," she said, beginning to load the plates into the dishwasher. "Their baby has been so sick, but Carol said he's better. This is the first night she and Stan have been out together in over two months."

When the dishes were loaded, Mark took Bev's hand. "Come in the den, honey. I saved my birthday present for you until we could be alone." Bev's eyes danced, and her face lit up with a smile. They playfully tugged each other into the den.

"Here you go," Mark said, handing his wife a flat package. "I can't wait to see how you like it." He sat down beside Bev on the sofa as she began to unwrap the gift.

"What could possibly be in such a thin box?" Bev asked, glancing slyly at her husband. From the package she pulled a large envelope and opened it. "Mark, these are plane tickets and reservations in Hawaii! I can't believe it! We're going to Hawaii? Oh, thank you, thank you!" Bev gave Mark a big hug, patting him on the back and the shoulders. She kissed him over and over. "I've *dreamed* of going to Hawaii for so long!"

"Me, too," Mark said, enjoying his wife's happiness. "It'll be the beginning of our new life together."

Bev suddenly stopped laughing and looked questioningly at Mark. "Our new life? What are you talking about?"

"You know, Bev. It's the beginning of our family. Remember how you've always said that you wanted to wait until you were 30 to begin having children? Well, you're 30 now. I'm ready if you are!" Mark smiled happily at Bev.

She turned slowly away, the joy draining out of her. She laid the tickets and reservations on the sofa. Standing up, Bev walked over to the fireplace and tapped her fingers on the mantle.

"Bev, what's the matter? You're scaring me." Mark went to his wife and tried to look at her face. Bev kept turning away. "Honey, what's going on?" Bev silently shook her head, biting her lip. She refused to meet his eyes.

Mark looked into the empty fireplace, then returned to the sofa. He collapsed on the soft cushions and sighed deeply. "Don't bother. I can guess. You don't want any kids now either."

Bev stood numbly, staring at the floor. The moments were thick with tension and unspoken feelings. Finally she broke the silence. "I'm sorry, but I just can't do it, Mark. I know I talked about having a baby when I was 30, but I don't feel any differently now than I did three years ago."

"And just how is it that you feel, Bev?" Mark said sarcastically. "Run it all by me once again. I seem to have forgotten all your wonderful reasons for refusing to bear my child."

"Oh, Mark, don't talk like that," Bev said, gingerly sitting on the rocking chair. "It's not the end of the world if we don't have children."

"It's the end of the world for *me*," Mark said. "I love kids and want some of my own. To me it's the whole purpose of marriage—to have a family."

"Oh, beautiful!" Bev said, her anger flaring. "Talk about a nearsighted focus! For your information, marriage is much more than having babies. You're an intelligent man, Mark. How can you be so stupid about this?"

"Who are you calling stupid?" Mark yelled, jumping to his feet. "What's stupid, what's *disgusting,* is how you keep changing your mind! When we were married, you talked about having children, but you kept putting it off. You keep changing. That's not fair, Bev. You knew going into this marriage that I wanted kids."

"And you knew I had other things to do."

"Yes, but you led me to believe that the day would come when those things would be over and you'd be a mother to my children. You said that when you were 30 you'd be ready."

"Well, I'm *not*. I thought I would be but I'm not. I have a career I love, I have opportunities for advancement and for travel, and I have no desire for a child." Bev's eyes were level with Mark's when she rose and faced him. "Besides, I look at my friends and how tied down they are with their kids, and I remember my mother and how she gave her whole life just to raise children, and I don't want any part of it. I have one life, Mark, just one. And I have a whole bunch of things I want to do with it. And taking care of babies and raising kids isn't one of them." Bev squared her shoulders, nodded her head sharply and stormed out of the den.

Mark watched her go, his eyes blazing. Breathing heavily, he started after his wife but stopped at the doorway. He leaned on the doorpost, shaking his head, muttering to himself.

Half an hour later Bev returned to the den. She'd changed into her lounging robe and had brushed her hair. The anger was gone. She was very pale.

Mark was sitting in the large armchair, facing the fireplace. He'd built a blazing fire and was studying the dancing flames.

"We've got to talk," Bev said quietly. "OK?"

Mark nodded, continuing to stare into the fire.

Bev turned the rocker to face Mark. "I'm sorry for getting so angry. You don't know how I've been dreading this very scene. I've even been dreading my 30th birthday, knowing this was coming."

Mark looked at his wife. His eyes were red and puffy. "I'm sorry, too. I didn't mean for this to happen. I'm sorry your birthday was spoiled."

"It's OK. We have to talk about this, Mark. It's better that we get it out. May I please tell you how I feel? I really do have some solid reasons for not wanting to have children."

"I'd like to know what they are," Mark said.

"Please listen to all of them, Mark. Then I'll be happy to listen to your reasons." Bev took a deep breath and slowly let it out. "First of all, I think about my mother. She literally died in her tracks taking care of us four kids. She had nothing else in her life. I don't want to live like that, honey. And I really, truly do not feel suited to raise children. I could physically bear a child, but I don't think I have the capacity or patience to raise one. And I don't think it's fair to bring a child into the world when I don't really want one. That's a terrible thing to do to a child.

"There are social issues involved, too. I've told you before that I feel strongly about zero population growth and about the whole hunger issue. To me that says that I can help by not adding any more mouths or bodies to the face of this earth. And with the nuclear issue being what it is—well, I'm not sure I want to bring children into a society like this.

"As I said before, Mark, I have my career. I love teaching English at the college. I'm dealing with adults, which I thoroughly enjoy. I have chances for advancement. I know I could combine a career with parenting. I have friends who do just that. But they're wearing themselves out, and it seems to me that they aren't doing either job particularly well. I do have a choice in this day and age of birth control—and, Mark, I choose not to have children."

Mark sighed and nodded. "OK, I hear you. Now I want you to hear me." He shifted in his chair so he could face Bev. "First, I know that raising a family isn't all there is to marriage. That's too narrow, and I'm sorry."

"Thank you for that," Bev said softly.

"I love children, Bev. As you know, my family consisted of just me and my dad. I used to dream of having lots of kids around, and I still feel that way. I feel incomplete as a person without children of my own. I feel as if children are my legacy to the world. I can't imagine growing old and not having children and grandchildren around me. I'm beginning to think that we've gotten too self-centered, Bev. I find a big emphasis on the material things in our lives. I think focusing on children would be good for us as people, not just as husband and wife. I see my friends with their children, and I really envy them. Bev, I'd even be willing to give up my position at the junior high to stay home with the baby if you'd just agree to have one."

Bev's eyes were filled with tears. The flames looked shimmery and weird to her. "I don't know what to say, Mark. I can see how important this is to you."

"I don't know what to say either," Mark replied. "I realize you have very strong feelings about it."

The fire danced in the hearth. The grandfather clock solemnly ticked and tocked.

▪ Something to Talk About ▪

1. First make a case for choosing not to have children. Describe Bev's feelings and beliefs, and add other ideas you've felt yourself or heard from others.

2. Now make a case for choosing to have children. Describe Mark's feelings and beliefs, again adding others which you've experienced or know about.

3. What's going to happen to Bev and Mark? What do you think *should* happen? Why? What suggestions do you have for this couple?

4. If they decide not to have children, how could Mark satisfy his feelings of love and enjoyment for children? What sort of "legacy" could he leave?

5. If they decide to have children after all, how could Bev adjust and/or justify her feelings about personal and social issues?

6. Bev and Mark believe they are physically able to have children. What happens to a couple's relationship when they are unable to have children even when they want them? What happens to a relationship when more and more children are born, even when they're not particularly wanted?

7. In the light of modern medical developments such as birth control, genetic counseling, "test tube" conception, and implants of embryos, as well as such social phenomena as adoption, surrogate mothers, abortion, unwed parenthood by choice, and sperm banks, how does a couple make loving, responsible choices?

8. What message does the church have to give in this time of multiple choices in family planning? Contrast Gen. 1:28 with 1 John 4:7, Rom. 8:18-23, and Rom. 8:31, 38-39. What Christian teachings and concepts are applicable in situations like those described above? Why is there no one pat answer for every situation?

14

▪ When Violence and ▪ Abuse Erupt

The sun shone brightly into the small conference room, lighting up the quiet blue and green decor. Don stood by the window, watching the cars go in and out of the counseling center's parking lot. So much depended on this visit with Shirley. What would he do if she refused to come home? How would he live without Shirley or Steve? She *had* to come home, that was all. He'd convince her she *had* to.

"Your wife is here now, Don," the counselor said, coming in the open door. "I'll give you a half hour together before interrupting, but I'll be at the desk right outside the door if you want me to come in before that. Have a good visit."

The counselor closed the door. Shirley leaned on the wall right beside it, looking as if she might disappear any moment.

Don looked at Shirley with eager eyes. "You're thinner, sweetheart. Haven't you been eating? Aren't they feeding you right at that place?"

Shirley didn't look at him. "I'm OK. The food's good."

"How's Steve? Has he grown any?" Don began to move toward the conference table.

Shirley stiffened as he got closer to her. "Steve's fine."

Don sat down at the table and motioned to the chair beside him. "Come on, Shirley, sit down so we can talk."

Shirley walked to the other side of the table, seating herself opposite her husband. The table was big and solid. "How are you?"

"I'm OK," Don answered. "Busy, of course. I've been working almost every day, and I've been in lots of counseling sessions here at the center."

"Oh? Are you getting any help?" Shirley looked her husband directly in the face for the first time in a month. His eyes were clear, and he was smiling at her. "You're looking good."

"I'm better, Shirley, I really am. And I want you to come home right away."

"I—I don't think so, Don. I'm not ready yet."

"Aw, honey, it's been a whole month. I'm not going to hit you anymore, I swear. I was just off my head for a while, that's all. It's not going to happen again." Don spoke earnestly.

"Yeah, well, you've said that before," Shirley answered. "Listen, Don, I feel safe and reasonably happy at the women's shelter. Steve and I are going to stay there until I feel better about things. Then—I don't know what I'm going to do."

A pang of fear struck Don's stomach. "What do you mean, you don't know? You'll come back to our house, that's what!"

"Not necessarily. You've hurt me too many times, Don. I took it from you for five years—all the time we've been married. This last time you almost killed me, do you realize that?" Shirley's voice was strong and accusing.

"Oh, come on, it wasn't that bad," Don said, shaking his head and laughing a little. "You really have made too much of a few little slaps."

Shirley stood up and glared down at her husband. "There you go again, minimizing your ugly and abusive treatment of me! Don Walters, this last attack of yours gave me a black eye, a brain concussion, internal bleeding, and huge bruises on my breasts and my back. My arm was out of its socket, and ligaments were torn. The doctors said that if I hadn't gotten treatment I would have hemorrhaged to death from the internal damage. I've had it with you and your so-called love taps!"

"All right, all *right*," Don said. "Sit down, will you? You're right, I know I hurt you. I don't know why I said that. This is one of the things I've been doing in therapy—admitting to myself that I really do hurt you. And I think I'm starting to figure out why I do it."

Shirley slowly sat down, staring at the man across from her. "Oh? Why do you do it?"

Don glanced at his wife and looked away. "It's hard to talk about. I'm embarrassed about it."

Shirley didn't say anything. She stared at Don until he squirmed uneasily.

"Look, Shirl. It's hard to admit that I need anyone, but I do. I need *you*. I'm so afraid you'll leave me. I'm always worried about it. I guess I do things to get you to stay with me." Don studied his hands.

Shirley's mouth hung open. "You hurt me so I'll stay with you?"

"I don't think of it that way. Somehow I think that if you see how fiercely I love you, you'll stay with me."

"And that includes chipping my teeth and knocking me unconscious?" Shirley asked incredulously.

Don shrugged. "It sounds stupid when you say it like that. You see, my counselor says I've never really grown up emotionally. I still treat problems like a kid would—throwing tantrums, using force before talking, all those things. I have to learn to handle problems and disappointments more maturely."

"That's got to be the understatement of the century!"

"I'm learning, sweetheart, I really am! I promise you I am. That's the reason I asked for this time with you," Don said, reaching for Shirley's hands across the table. She drew away. "I want to tell you I'm getting better."

Shirley got up and walked to the window. The parking lot was nearly empty. The van that had brought her from the shelter was parked near the front door.

"The other thing, Shirley, is that I'm starting to understand my background," Don said, watching her from his seat. "Remember how I told you about my folks, how they fought all the time and how they finally divorced? My counselor says that I learned these bad ways of dealing with problems as I was growing up and listening to my parents. My old man beat on my mother."

"And did you like that, Don?" Shirley said, whirling around. "Did it make you feel good, hearing your mother suffer?"

Don was startled by Shirley's ferocity. "No, no, of course not," he stammered. "I hated him for it. I wanted to hurt him the way he hurt her."

"All right," Shirley said, advancing toward him. "Just think what you're doing to Steve. That boy is four years old, Don. He's seen you beat me senseless. He's heard the screams at night when he's lying in his bed. He's felt the anger and fear and hatred in our house." She leaned on the table with her hands, staring at her husband. "How can you do that to your own son, knowing how hurt you were by your father doing the same thing? It's bad enough that you throw me around and beat me up, but how on God's earth can you treat your only son with such contempt?"

Don had never heard Shirley talk like this. She'd been so quiet and submissive before. He swallowed hard. The fear made him hot and dizzy.

Shirley removed her white-hot gaze from Don and returned to her seat. She waited for him to compose himself.

"I know you're right. I know I'm a rotten, hateful man." Don's voice was very low. He was slumped in his chair. "I'm so sorry—for everything."

Shirley took a deep breath and let it out slowly. "All right. I needed to hear you admit it, Don. Before, you've always been right, even when you were beating me with that club. Are you going to continue in therapy?"

Don wiped some stray tears off his cheeks. "Yeah, I have to continue. The court ordered six months of therapy, then a reevaluation and the possibility of even more after that. I got to tell you, Shirl, this therapy business is painful. But I know I'm better. And I'll do anything, *anything* to get you and Steve back home again."

"I've been in therapy, too. Did you know that?" Shirley glanced at Don who looked inquiringly at her. "I'm learning new ways of coping with problems too. You're not the only one who learned bad habits at home. My mother was overly submissive to my father. She was lucky he didn't physically hurt her, but he was very overbearing. I watched her take it all the time I was growing up, and I just figured that was how a wife acted. I'm learning how to assert myself now, Don. I'm not going to be the same person you married in that respect. I've found out I enjoy being in control of myself."

"Well, that's good," Don said uncertainly. "But that means you won't need me anymore, I guess."

"No, Don, that's not what it means," Shirley said. "I never realized you were so insecure about me. I always thought you were in charge and were the big *macho* guy. It just means that I'm a stronger person who refuses to be mistreated any longer. That will be good for any relationship I have, including marriage."

The counselor opened the door. "The center will be closing in 10 minutes. Shirley, will you be going back to the shelter or will you be going home?"

"I'll tell you in a few minutes, OK?" The counselor smiled and closed the door.

Shirley held out her hand. Don eagerly took it. They looked carefully into each other's eyes. Outside, the driver turned on the van's engine.

• Something to Talk About •

1. What do you think Shirley is going to do? Why? What do you think she *should* do? Why?

2. Describe Don and Shirley's marriage before the crisis a month ago. What habits had each of them learned in their parental homes regarding a marriage relationship?

3. What happened a month ago? What steps have been taken since then? How is Don feeling now? How is Shirley feeling? Have either or both of them changed? If so, how?

4. What future do you see for this marriage? What things need to happen to make it a successful marriage?

5. If you have known people in an abusive marriage, describe how they coped with it and with what results.

6. What resources are available in your community for couples in abusive and violent marriages? What can the church do to help families in these crises? What hope does the gospel bring?

15

▪ When a Couple Moves ▪ to a New Location

"Pass those pork chops, would you, Mona? You really made a great Sunday dinner! Isn't that right, Richie?" Dick grinned at his eight-year-old son who was eating the whipped cream off his Jello.

Ramona nodded her thanks. "It wasn't much trouble. I put the meat in the oven before we went to church."

"Anyway, as I was saying, my new job at the college is taking on dimensions I never anticipated. For instance, on Friday one of the history professors said, 'Dick, I've got an idea for a travel seminar that needs your skill at public relations to make it go.' See, he wants to organize a tour of the California missions."

Ramona poured another glass of milk for Richie. "Oh? That's nice."

"And he even suggested I might like to go along on the tour. Naturally I asked if you could go, too, and he said we could probably work something out." Dick smiled broadly at Ramona, then realized she wasn't listening. "Mona, did you hear anything I said?"

Startled, Ramona quickly replied, "Oh—right! Sounds good." But Dick could tell by her expressionless eyes that she was just mouthing words, saying what she thought he wanted to hear.

"OK, let's have it." Dick wasn't smiling anymore, and his voice had an edge to it. "Are you still sulking about moving here? Are we going to have to go through all that again?"

"Dick, you just don't understand. You didn't understand in Oregon, and you don't understand in California."

"Then tell me what I don't understand. Come on, let's have it. Tell me how heartless I am to move you to a town where you don't know anyone. Tell me how mean I am to take you away from your friends. Come on, make me understand."

"You know perfectly well that you don't *want* to understand. I told you in Oregon how I felt, but would you listen? Oh, no. You just went ahead and did what you wanted to do. Since when did your job mean more than your family's happiness?"

"Mona, that's not fair. We talked the job offer over many times. And you always said it sounded wonderful."

"Wonderful for *you*! I told you how I felt about leaving everything I've ever known. What's in California for me? Just you and Richie, and you're gone most of the time, and Richie's in school. It's not fun being alone, Dick—especially when I know I have friends in Oregon."

Dick sighed heavily and rubbed his hand over his face. "All right, now listen, Mona. Don't you remember how happy and optimistic you were as we were leaving Oregon? Remember how you said that everything was going to be great in California and that we'd have a beautiful new life?"

"Yeah, well, I thought everything *was* going to be fine. I expected people to welcome us, to come over and be friendly. I've never moved to a new community before, Dick. On TV neighbors are friendly to newcomers. In this town they don't seem to care. And *you've* seemed to change, too."

"Me? I haven't changed! *You've* changed! It's no picnic for me to come home to your sad face."

"And it's no picnic to have you talking about your job all the time, Dick. You do, you know. I'm really tired of hearing about all the people you meet and all the interesting things you do."

"See here, Mona. Starting a new job is a lot of hard work. Do you have any idea how much strain and tension I'm under at the college? I have to learn to know all kinds of new people, not to mention all the new procedures. A little help and encouragement from you would be very welcome." Dick stood up abruptly from the table. "Aw, forget it. If you want to be in Oregon so much, why don't you just go on back."

Richie started to cry. "I don't want to go back to Oregon. I've got a rabbit here, and I love my teacher!"

"Now see what you've done," Ramona hissed at Dick as she gathered the boy into her arms. "It's OK, Richie. I'm sorry you had to hear all those bad words. Mommy and daddy are just trying to figure out what to do in our new place. Don't worry, it's OK, baby." Richie sobbed into her shoulder as Ramona glared at Dick over the boy's head.

Dick stalked out of the kitchen. A moment later the car door slammed and tires squealed down the driveway. The Sunday afternoon had just fallen apart.

The sun was slanting deeply into the covered patio when Dick came back. Ramona was lying rigidly on the chaise lounge. Without opening her eyes she said, "I was worried about you."

Dick settled into one of the cushioned redwood chairs and was silent for a few moments. "I had to get away. Hearing Richie cry made me crazy."

"I know, but he's OK. I sat with him for a while, and now he's listening to the records grandma sent."

"I had a chance to think a little, Mona. Why are we doing this to each other? We need to be close during these hard times of adjustment, but we keep snapping at each other."

Ramona sat on the edge of the chaise, facing her husband. "I know. I feel terrible about it. I'm sorry I said those things to you, Dick. It's just that I'm hurting inside, and you're the only one I have to talk to. I love you with all my heart, and I love Richie the same way, but Dick, I'm lonesome, so *lonesome*. You're busy with your job, and it hurts."

"I can see that it does. I just feel helpless, Mona. I can't live both our lives. I can't take you to work with me."

"Of course not, and I wouldn't want it that way. It helps when we can talk, Dick. That gives me strength."

A hummingbird hovered around the feeder. The little bird persistently sipped the red sugar water, its head darting back and forth. Then it suddenly zipped over the roof and out of sight.

"Mona, I think we're going to have to be a little more aggressive ourselves."

"What do you mean, aggressive? You know I can't just go up to a stranger and start talking. I've never been able to do that."

"No, not that. But look at that hummingbird. He's back again and working hard to get his supper out of that feeder. He has to go to the feeder, Mona. The juice doesn't go to him. Maybe we have to do something that brings us toward the people in this town. We could sit here for a long time if we wait for people to come to us."

"I really thought they would, Dick. But you're probably right. Well, any ideas?"

Suddenly Dick got up and went into the house. A moment later he was back with the Sunday church bulletin. "I thought I remembered seeing this announcement. They're looking for a Cubmaster and some den mothers to start a church-sponsored Cub Scout troop. Richie is just about the right age for Cub Scouts, and I used to be a Boy Scout. You're real good with kids. Maybe this is something we could do to get acquainted. Just think of all the families we'd meet in a group like this."

"In Oregon we never would have had time for it, what with all our other activities, but here—" Mona's voice had some enthusiasm in it, Dick noticed.

"Let's talk to the pastor and see if anyone else has indicated interest in starting a troop," Dick suggested.

Ramona was suddenly struck by a thought. "Wait, wait a minute, Dick. We'd better ask Richie about all this. What if he doesn't want to be a Cub Scout? That would shoot the whole idea."

"Let's go ask him." Dick grabbed Ramona's hand, and they went to find Richie.

After the 11 o'clock news, Dick and Ramona began to prepare for bed.

"So the pastor was excited about our offer?" Ramona knew the answer, but she wanted to hear Dick tell the story again.

"You bet he was! He said that we're an answer to prayer. Can you believe that? All our stewing and fighting turn out to be someone's answer to prayer."

"I'll call those two women—Alice and Margaret—in the morning. I think I'll invite them over for coffee, and then we can find a time to get together with you. Maybe we could have a barbeque out on the patio and invite their husbands to come." Ramona began to think about the menu.

"Great idea! And I'll call the Scouting office tomorrow and see what the procedures are. Come here, beautiful." Dick hugged Ramona. "We're going to make it, you know. And we're going to do it together."

Ramona relaxed in Dick's arms. She felt so warm and safe. "I think it'll be fun. Did you see the smile on Richie's face when you told him he could be a Cub Scout?"

Dick laughed and hugged his wife even closer. "You bet I did! That smile lit up every corner of my heart."

▪ Something to Talk About ▪

1. Dick and Ramona are at a crisis point in their marriage. Describe the situation.

2. How is Dick feeling? How is Ramona feeling? Where does the conflict come? What is happening to their marriage?

3. What things are they doing to make the adjustment easier? Name at least four things. What suggestions do you have for them?

4. Have you ever moved to a new community? How did you feel? What things did you do to make the adjustment easier? What did other people do to help you?

5. Think of what it might be like to be a newcomer in your community. How can you help people make the adjustment? What can the church do for newcomers?

16

▪ When Unfaithfulness ▪
Results in Disease

The screaming and crying had been over for an hour. Karen rocked herself incessantly in the antique rocker in the living room. Mike, slouched in a chair in the den, stared without seeing at the TV.

The words full of accusation and pain had flown for a long time. Karen's suspicions of Mike's unfaithfulness had suddenly become reality during her visit to Dr. Sullivan. The fever she had had for a week along with the pounding headache wasn't just the flu or a nasty cold. The doctor said those symptoms combined with the painful blisters on her genitals confirmed a case of herpes, type two. Since Mike was her only sexual partner, Karen knew he must have slept with someone else, who had infected him with herpes. Dr. Sullivan had tried to calm her, pointing out that the disease, while difficult and incurable as yet, was not life-threatening and that both she and Mike would be free of symptoms most of the time. But it wasn't just the disease that sickened and infuriated Karen. It was the fact that Mike had lied to her about his activities while on the road with his job, that he'd been unfaithful to her. It was the fact that he had infected her with the disease some *hooker* had given him.

What to do? That was the question for Karen. She rocked and rocked, many thoughts spinning around in her head. She was angry, so very angry. She also was in shock. It was absolutely unbelievable that this was happening to her, to them. Karen was frightened, too. This awful disease—what was it going to do to her? Would she pass it on to the children? It was like she now was branded *unclean, unclean*. Karen had heard her friends talk about herpes: "It's incurable, you know." "People who sleep around get it!" And besides all that, Karen was sick and miserable. The doctor had given her some medication, but he had said herpes was a virus and would run its course. The first attack usually lasted about three weeks. Karen's head pounded. She knew her fever must have risen again during the battle with Mike. What to do, what to do?

What was going to happen? That was the question for Mike. The absolute worst things he had imagined had actually happened. Karen had found out about his one-night stands, and she had gotten herpes from him. Mike wanted to die. Anything else seemed too good for him. He had lived in fear of this very moment ever since he discovered he himself had herpes. Mike had seen a doctor in Seattle, who explained the illness to him and prescribed some medication. He'd been able to hide the illness from Karen when he got home, saying he had the flu. Now would Karen leave him? Would she take the kids? Guilty and depressed, Mike hid his face in his hands and sobbed. Maybe he should just kill himself and end the misery. Then Karen would be free of him, and he'd be free of the pain. But Mike lacked the energy to seriously pursue suicide. What was going to happen, what was going to happen?

Tony and Meg came home from school promptly at 3:30 P.M. Karen had roused herself enough to put cookies and milk on the table for their snack. She didn't hug them, but tried to smile brightly as they excitedly told her their news.

"Sharon's having a pizza party tonight, mom, and she's invited all the kids in our class. We're supposed to bring our records, and it's going to last until 10 o'clock. Please can we go? Please, please? Everyone's going to be there!"

Karen laughed at the twins despite herself. Who could resist those funny kids when they turned on the charm? Besides, Sharon's house was just down the block, and it would give them something to do tonight while she wrestled with this awful situation. "Sure, go ahead. Just be home by 10, not a minute later."

Mike heard the kids racing down the hall, laughing about an old joke he remembered from his own childhood. What innocence those kids have, he thought bitterly. If only *he* could start over.

Sometime after seven Karen appeared in the doorway of the den. Mike was resting his head on the back of the chair, his eyes closed. A newscaster was explaining the crisis in South Africa to Mike's unhearing ears. Karen turned the TV off. Mike opened his eyes.

"OK, Mike. We have to talk." Karen sat on the edge of the sofa.

Mike looked at her dully. He knew what was coming. She was leaving, taking the twins with her to her mother's house. A shuddering sigh involuntarily racked him.

"I've been doing a lot of thinking, Mike. I need to know some things. Will you tell me the truth?"

"Sure." *There's nothing more to lose,* Mike thought wearily. "Why not?"

"Why did you sleep with those—those women?" Karen's voice was so low Mike could barely make out the words. But they were plain enough. He started to sob.

"I don't know, I don't *know*! I guess I was lonesome. It seemed like such a *macho* thing to do! It was so stupid! I can't believe how *stupid* I was! I'm so sorry. I wish I could do

everything over again, somehow make it all right for you."
The tears were taking over. Mike couldn't get any more words
out. Karen was crying now too.

Minutes slid by while both wept. Mike stood up to get his
handkerchief out of his pocket. He blew his nose loudly. Karen
looked like a small child crying her heart out. The sight of her
broke Mike's heart. He sat on the sofa and gathered Karen
into his arms. Surprisingly she didn't resist but wept into his
shirt. He tried to comfort her by caressing her hair and patting
her shoulder. "Just cry, baby. Let it all come out," he said
brokenly.

Gradually the sobbing quieted, and the two of them rocked
in each other's arms. Mike was afraid to move. He didn't want
to break the spell of the moment.

"Mike?" Karen's voice was muffled, but Mike heard the
plaintive note.

"Yes?"

"What did the doctor tell you about herpes?"

Mike gently released Karen and held her so he could see her
face. She looked drained and miserable. "Well, he said it's a
virus that is in epidemic stages. He said about 20 million Amer-
icans have it." Karen shuddered and hid her face in his shoulder
again. Mike held her closely, grateful she would let him touch
her. "He also said that as yet there's no cure, but that scientists
the world over are looking for one. In the meantime we have
to live with it. But he said that with rest and with as little
stress as possible, further attacks can be kept at a minimum.
Some people have very few further attacks."

Karen was quiet now. She felt as if there weren't any tears
left in her body. Utterly tired, she drew back from Mike and
rested against the sofa. "Mike, my first thought was that I had
to leave you, to get far, far away. And I still may have to do
that. I don't know. But my doctor told me about a family
counselor right there in his building. Dr. Sullivan said he always recommends immediate counseling in cases like ours. At

first I didn't even want to think about it. I just wanted to get away. But after seeing the kids, and after thinking a little bit, I guess I'd like to try some counseling anyway. Would you be willing to go?"

Mike could hardly believe his ears. "Of course I'll go! I've been hoping and praying all afternoon that something would happen to give me a chance, but I didn't really think it would. Oh, Karen, I'm so desperately sorry—for everything. I wish I could undo it all and start over."

"I know. So do I. And mind you, I'm not saying this will be the answer, Mike," Karen warned. "I need time, and I need answers. I also need to talk this thing out with people who know something about it. Mike, I need to know if I can ever trust you again. Right now I don't see how I can."

Mike nodded. His heart was sinking again. He should have known it wouldn't be so easy. "Who will you talk to?"

Karen sighed. She rubbed some drying tears from her face. "I'm not sure. I know I should talk to Pastor Clark, but I don't know if I can. I heard there's a woman pastor over at Grace. Maybe I could talk to her about this."

"Maybe you could talk to your friend, Elaine."

"Oh, no, never! I've heard her talk about herpes before, and she'd never understand."

"Karen—"

"I'm not going to leave tonight or even tomorrow, Mike, if that's what you're wondering. I probably should, but I don't even have the energy to try. Maybe something good will come out of this. Maybe there'll be a miracle."

▪ Something to Talk About ▪

1. What is happening to Karen and Mike's marriage? Describe the problems they're facing.

2. Describe how Karen is feeling. Look at the situation from Mike's point of view and describe his feelings. Is any communication taking place?

3. Karen and Mike need help right now. What kinds of help can you suggest? Why do you think Karen didn't want to talk to Pastor Clark? What message does the church have to give to Karen and Mike? What help might be forthcoming from the church?

4. Do you know of situations similar to this one? What measures proved to be helpful? What do you think will happen to Karen and Mike? How would you react, what would you do, in a similar situation?

5. What do you know about the disease herpes? If this is a new or unfamiliar illness to you, ask some questions. What have you learned about it from this story?

6. Some cities have HELP chapters which are a part of the national group, The Herpes Resource Center, located in Palo Alto, California. The chapters are support groups for herpes sufferers. What other groups might be helpful?

17

▪ When a Couple's ▪ Priorities Are Distorted

Soft radio music filled the room. The late afternoon sunlight danced and twinkled through the window and the Peter Pan mobile. In the middle of the floor, surrounded by music and sunlight, Alice rocked her son as she read to him.

" 'And the little boy called his dog. "Here, Rusty! Come here, boy!" The dog ran out of the field and toward Michael, barking as he ran!' " Alice rubbed the child's tummy and chest as she read.

The door opened abruptly, and Roger stuck his head into the room. "Hi! I'm home. Everybody OK?"

"Oh, hi, honey," Alice answered, smiling. "We're just fine. I'm reading Robbie his favorite story, the one about Michael and his dog Rusty. We're almost to the best part, when Rusty saves Michael from the rushing river."

"Right," Roger said. "I'm home for about an hour, Alice. Then I have to leave again for the Indian Princess meeting with Peggy. Shall I make dinner?"

Alice had turned back to Robbie and the book. "It's already in the oven. I'll come out as soon as Robbie's sleeping. Let's see now, Robbie, where were we?"

"Alice, I really should talk to you before I leave again," Roger said. "There's something I've got to tell you."

" 'Michael cried, "Help me, Rusty! Help me!" And the dog tried to reach his master.' " Alice was once again absorbed in the story, patting her son's tummy.

Roger's mouth set in an exasperated expression. He watched his wife rocking his son, the son who only stared vacantly. Alice's voice was rich and full as she read the story. She stimulated the child's muscles with her hands and rocked with a firm, regular cadence. Roger tried to get her attention. "Alice, how long do you think it'll be? It's important that I talk to you." But Alice continued to read and rock. The boy stared, his mouth open, his muscles limp. Roger closed the door.

Forty-five minutes later Alice appeared in the kitchen. Peggy and Roger were eating the overdone tuna casserole. "Oh, why aren't you eating the salad with the casserole? And the nice rolls?" Alice hurried to the refrigerator and pulled out the gelatin salad. "Here, this goes with the casserole," she said, spooning some gelatin on Peggy's plate. "Here, Roger, don't you want some?" Alice put the salad on the table and hurried to get the rolls.

"I really don't care for any now," Roger said, folding his napkin. "I've eaten as much dinner as I want. I didn't know you had all that prepared. I just found the dish in the oven."

Alice settled at the table, letting out a deep breath as she relaxed. "It took longer with Robbie than I'd anticipated. Usually he goes right to sleep after I've read to him, but tonight he kept his eyes open. Roger, I think he's trying to talk to me." Alice put the remaining portion of casserole on her plate and began to eat.

Roger gave his wife an unbelieving look. "Oh, come on."

"No, really. I think I see him trying to form words. Didn't you notice it this afternoon, Peggy? You were with me when he tried to say, 'mommy.' Tell daddy what you saw."

Peggy glanced at her father. Her nine-year-old face was uncertain. "Well, he moved his tongue a little bit."

"There, you see?" Alice said triumphantly. "Peggy saw it, too."

"Alice, Robbie always moves his tongue. It's the one thing he *does* move. That doesn't mean he's trying to talk."

"That's where you're wrong, honey. I'm sure it means something."

Roger stood up. "Are you ready, Peggy? We've got to leave for your Indian Princess meeting." He dropped his napkin on the table and headed for the hall closet.

"Oh, Roger," Alice called after her husband. "Did I hear you say you wanted to talk to me about something?"

"Forget it," Roger's voice said from the front hall. "I'll talk to you later. Come on, Peggy."

"Good-bye, mom," the girl said, leaving half her dinner on the plate. "Dad and I have a part in the program tonight."

"You do? My goodness, why didn't you tell me about it? I could have taken Robbie to the program." Alice's voice trailed off when she heard the front door slam. She stared at her plate. The casserole was cold, sticky, and unappetizing. Alice sighed and began clearing the dishes from the table. She ate a few spoonfuls of gelatin and a roll while standing at the counter. The food sat like a lump in her stomach.

Shrill screams pierced the quietness. Alice ran down the hall and into Robbie's room. The child lay on his back, staring at the ceiling, screaming rhythmically. Alice gathered him up in her arms and settled into the rocker. "It's OK, Robbie," she soothed the staring, screaming child. "Mommie's here now." Rock, rock. Soothe, soothe. It was a familiar pattern. Alice had been doing this for five years. Robbie hadn't breathed for 10 minutes following his birth, despite all the efforts of the doctors. His brain damage apparently was due both to the lack of oxygen and a congenital problem. No one knew all the causes, but Robbie was severely brain-damaged. And Alice's life was spent taking care of him and hoping for improvement.

Alice was still rocking Robbie when Roger and Peggy returned. They tiptoed into the bedroom, smiles on their faces. "Oh, mommie, it was great!" Peggy whispered. "Dad and I won second place, and we got a prize." Alice nodded at them, smiling. Robbie started screaming again. Roger and Peggy quickly backed out of the room. Alice rocked and rocked.

At midnight Alice crawled into bed. Roger was watching "The Tonight Show," his head propped on the pillows. "The show's all done, just as you get here," Roger said. "I'll turn the set off, and we can talk." He reached over and flicked the switches for both the TV and the light. Darkness fell around them like a soft blanket. "Robbie finally went to sleep, did he?"

"Finally. I rocked him for five hours. He's sleeping out of sheer exhaustion now. That's what I'm going to be doing in about one minute." Alice's voice was weary.

"Alice, I know this isn't the best time to talk to you, but there doesn't seem to be any good time. It's almost impossible to talk to you alone." Roger spoke hesitantly. "Is it OK if I tell you something now? I know you're tired."

"This is fine," Alice said in the darkness. "I've been wanting to talk to you too. Robbie really needs to be evaluated again. It's been almost a year since we had him to New York, and the specialist there thought he could tell more about Robbie when he was six. He'll be six in a few months so I was thinking—"

"Alice," Roger said, trying to break in. "Alice, please."

"And I really do think there's been progress since the last time we were in New York. I told you this afternoon that he seems to be trying to talk, but what I didn't tell you is that I think he'll be crawling soon. Every now and again he seems to move his legs in such a way that it seems like crawling."

"Alice! Be quiet!" Roger whispered hoarsely. "I've got something to say to you." He shook Alice's shoulder to get her complete attention.

"What is it?" Alice said. "What can be so important to take the place of Robbie? Our son is the most important thing in our—"

"I'm leaving you, Alice!"

The silence echoed Roger's words. Alice lay very still. "What?"

"I said, I'm leaving you. I'm very sorry, but I can't keep up this charade any longer. I've found someone else, and I want to make a new life—with her." Roger swallowed hard. "I'm sorry. I've been wanting to tell you for a couple months. There never was a right time. I'll leave in the morning."

"You're leaving me and the children?" Alice's voice was faint and distant.

"I'll make very good financial arrangements. You won't have to worry. Alice, you're so wrapped up in Robbie that you'll hardly miss me. I'm just concerned about Peggy. I may ask to have custody of Peggy. You don't pay enough attention to her."

"You won't take my daughter. I guarantee you that."

Roger fell back on his pillow and groaned. "Don't you see, Alice? Our marriage has been a sham, a *pretense,* for five years. I've begged you to put Robbie in a care facility or a foster home. We have no marriage left, no home, no family life to speak of. You've given yourself completely to that child, who doesn't even know who you are." Roger folded his arms across his eyes.

Alice jerked herself out of bed. "That's not true! I'm his mother and he knows it. It's *you*! All you want is fun and games. When things have gotten tough, you've run off. You don't help me. You don't care anything about us. Go ahead—

leave! Leave tonight. Leave right now." She ran out of the bedroom and down the hall toward Robbie's room.

Roger wept in gigantic, hoarse sobs. "Why won't you listen to me? Why can't you hear me? I need you just as much as Robbie does."

• Something to Talk About •

1. Describe Alice's priorities. Do you feel she is justified in choosing them? What, if any, adjustments would you recommend?

2. Describe where Roger's priorities lie. Do you feel he is justified? What, if any, adjustments would you recommend?

3. Describe the marriage relationship that has resulted from these priority choices. Evaluate the amount and type of communication taking place between Alice and Roger. How have the priority choices affected the communication?

4. What's going to happen to this marriage? If you were a marriage counselor whom Alice and Roger consulted following this story, how would you try to help them? What suggestions might you make regarding priority choices and communication in marriage?

5. This story focuses on two priorities that have become distorted: a brain-damaged child and the husband-wife relationship. Note that in and of themselves, both priorities are good. How have they become distorted? What other circumstances or emphases could become distorted priorities? Be sure to examine priority situations from the experiences and points of view of both husband and wife.

6. In a Christian marriage Christ is to be the central priority for both partners. What difference does it make when Christ is the priority rather than a person's particular interest or concern? Read Galatians 5:22-23 to discover the characteristics of a person led by God's Spirit. How does the "fruit of the Spirit" relate to this story or to any marriage situation involving priority choices?

18

▪ When a Couple's Child ▪ Is in Trouble

"I hate you, old man! I hate you!" Becky screamed as John held on to her arm. "Let me go. I can do what I want to—anything I want to." With a frantic effort Becky broke her father's grip and ran out the front door.

"Becky, come back here," John yelled as he chased his 16-year-old daughter across the lawn. But the sleek white car with the well-dressed man at the wheel was already in motion when Becky slammed and locked the door.

Shelley stood on the steps, her hands covering her mouth, her eyes wide with fear. The tears flowed unheeded down her cheeks, spilling over her fingers. She watched her husband slowly turn and walk back toward her. The anguish in his eyes was unbearable.

"Thank God, Bonnie and Jimmy weren't here to see that," he groaned. "What are we going to do, Shelley? What are we going to do?" John kept brushing giant tears away, but they immediately reappeared.

Shelley put her arms around John, murmuring comforting words. Becky had run away before, but never had it been this ugly. Usually she disappeared after school or in the middle of the night, sometimes taking her mother's car. She would be gone many days at a time and then would suddenly reappear. The police had brought her home sometimes, having found her spaced out on drugs and wandering the streets. Other times she'd been arrested on suspicion of selling illegal substances. Becky had been to psychologists, doctors, pastors, and counselors, but the end result was always the same: Becky refused to cooperate and continued her drug use. The last time Becky was arrested, the juvenile magistrate had suggested that a foster home might be the answer. John and Shelley had strongly opposed such a drastic step, but everything was going from bad to worse. This time Becky's drug dealer had come to pick her up.

"I'm going to kill that guy," John vowed. "I swear, I'm going to kill him for what he's done to Becky." Just saying his daughter's name caused the tears to pour forth once again.

"I know, I know," Shelley said. "I can't believe he actually showed up here. I think Becky called him, trying to embarrass us in the neighborhood. She was angry because we wouldn't give her the money she wanted."

"She just would have spent it on drugs. Besides, I didn't have $50 to give her. I offered her $5 so she could get her lunches next week at school, but she threw it at me and said she had to have the $50. Shelley, I love that girl, but I hate her, too. Sometimes I wish she'd never been born!" John cried out.

Shelley held him closely, but her heart was thudding in fear. She'd never heard John say that before. And she'd never heard him threaten anyone with death. What was happening to them? Dear God, what could they do?

At the dinner table Bonnie was inquisitive. "Isn't daddy going to eat with us, mom? And where's Becky?" the 10-year-old girl asked. Jimmy, eight years old, dug into his spaghetti.

"Dad's very tired tonight. He'll eat later," Shelley said as brightly as she could. "Becky's out for a while."

"Did she run away again?" Bonnie demanded. "Because if she did, I'm glad."

"Yeah," Jimmy echoed. "I'm glad, too."

Out of the corner of her eye Shelley saw John standing in the doorway. His voice was rough. "What do you mean, you're glad?"

"Because things are terrible around here when she's home. She makes all kinds of trouble for me and Jimmy. Becky even stole Jimmy's money from his bank."

"Yeah, $40. She took it all and didn't give it back," the little boy said dolefully. "I was saving that for my new bike."

"And she says weird things about 'needles' and 'smack' and 'angel dust,' mom," Bonnie continued. "I tell her she's crazy, but she just laughs and says a lot of dirty words. I cover my ears, but I can still hear her. I don't want to share a room with Becky anymore. I *hate* being with her!"

"Me, too," echoed Jimmy.

John stood perfectly still in the doorway. Shelley tried to reassure the children. "All right, Bonnie, I'll do something about it. And I'll get your money back, too, Jimmy. Everything's going to be fine, don't you worry." But her stomach had developed a deep pit.

John slowly walked out of the kitchen and into the living room. He sank into his favorite chair. When the children went to the den to watch television, John was staring at the large family portrait hanging over the sofa.

Shelley came in, settling into the other chair. "Are you all right, John?"

"Yeah, I'm OK. I'm just hearing voices, that's all."

"What? You're hearing voices?"

John nodded, still staring at the portrait. "Lots and lots of voices. Like your voice when we were married, promising that you'd love and cherish me in sickness and in health, in the good times and in the rugged times."

Shelley smiled despite herself. "That's what you promised me, too, John."

"And I can hear the kids' voices when they were small. Life was so simple then, wasn't it, Shelley? We never had to worry about where they were at night. We knew Becky was in her pretty canopy bed, and the other two were in their cribs." John sighed deeply and was quiet for a few moments, remembering. "But the loudest voices I'm hearing are the ones telling us that we have to take control of our lives and of our home and of our children."

"Like Dr. Panning and Pastor Eggers and the school psychologist," Shelley said.

"Yes, and like that juvenile counselor at the welfare office. I could have slugged that guy when he said we needed to help ourselves, but he was right."

"How on God's earth do we do that, John?"

The clock's ticking was very loud in the silence. Finally John said, "Pastor Eggers has been insisting that you and I must make specific ground rules for Becky, that we must agree on them, and that we must stick to our guns."

Shelley stood up abruptly and looked out the picture window, her back to her husband. "I've got to tell you, John, I really blame you for being too harsh with Becky. She needed you to love her more."

"You can't blame me anymore than I blame myself, Shelley. I know I've made mistakes. But you're not totally innocent either. I've told you time and again that you've been far too lenient with her. Becky needed you to be consistently firm."

Shelley whirled around to face John. Her expression was set and angry. "You just don't understand what it's been like. I've tried and I've tried." Shelley stopped suddenly, her shoulders sagged. Her head dropped and she sighed. "I don't want to fight about this anymore, John. We've both made mistakes with Becky, but that's past. We've got to face the problem and deal with it right now."

"That means we've got to take charge of this house. As it is, Becky is calling all the shots. She's got us jumping around like puppets," John said. "We need to do what Pastor Eggers suggested—lay out ground rules that Becky will have to obey if she's to continue living here."

"And if she refuses to follow the ground rules?"

"Shelley, this is the watershed point for our family. We've sat in the muck and mire long enough. We have to concentrate on Bonnie and Jimmy. We can't let Becky and all her problems destroy them. And if that means she must live elsewhere, so be it. You've said yourself that God can use even the worst problem for good. Well, I think we've got to trust him. We can try to keep Becky here at home with our ground rules and as much love as she'll accept, but if it doesn't work out, we'll have to be ready for the next step, tough as it may be."

Shelley nodded. "I know you're right. I'm so tired of being afraid of my own daughter. And after hearing what Bonnie said tonight, we have to concentrate on salvaging what we can. John, I'm so afraid. I'm afraid for Becky, but I'm afraid for us too. How much strain can our marriage take?"

John stood up and enveloped his wife in a hug. "We're OK, honey. If we didn't have a good marriage, it would have cracked long before this. And taking charge of this situation together is going to bring us even closer, you'll see."

"Another thing Pastor Eggers said was that we could get help from other parents who have had kids in trouble. I don't know about you," Shelley said, "but I've been so embarrassed about having a junkie for a daughter that I couldn't bring myself to talk to anyone but the doctor and the pastor. Maybe it's time that we start finding out what other parents have done."

"That sounds great to me. Why don't you call the pastor in the morning?"

"And I've been thinking that my sewing room could be made into a nice little bedroom for Bonnie. She could help make it real cute," Shelley said.

"That's terrific! Why didn't I think of that?" John enthused. "OK, let's sit at the table to start working out the ground rules. Our ground rule is that we have to agree about each one. Then let's get Bonnie and Jimmy involved in our plans about the bedroom and the new rules. Let's start acting like a family."

John went to his desk to gather paper and pencils. Shelley gazed out the picture window. Where was Becky and what was she doing?

▪ Something to Talk About ▪

1. Briefly describe the situation in this family. What problems is Becky having? What is this doing to her parents? to her brother and sister?

2. Make a list of the feelings and emotions John and Shelley are experiencing as a result of this situation. (There are at least eight.) Describe what specifically has caused each of these feelings.

3. What's happening to John and Shelley's marriage in this crisis? How are they feeling about each other? Why would trouble with a child affect a marriage relationship?

4. What positive signs do you find in this story? What other positive steps could you suggest to John and Shelley? If you were writing the ground rules for Becky, what would they be?

5. If you or someone close to you has had a child in trouble, share the feelings and what was done to help the situation. What positive or negative things happened to the marriage?

6. Help had been sought from the pastor as well as doctors and counselors. How did these people help? Note that the results of the counseling were not instantaneous. What help will other parents of troubled children be able to give John and Shelley? What other avenues of help do you know about?

19

• When a Couple Is Divided • over Religion

"Mommy, have I been baptized?" Lisa looked inquiringly at Elsa as they checked the napkin holders and condiment trays on all the tables. It was almost time to open the restaurant for the Sunday noon trade.

"Whatever makes you ask that question?" Elsa said, pouring ketchup into a plastic bottle.

"Sarah invited me to her Sunday school class today," Lisa answered. "The teacher was talking about how people are saved and go to heaven. She said you went to heaven if you're baptized, so I want to know if I'm baptized."

Elsa bit her lip. Why did Brian always manage to be gone when Lisa asked these difficult questions? When she was seven, she had asked where babies came from right in front of a bunch of customers. Now at 10 she was asking about religion. As usual, Brian was safely out of the restaurant.

"Well?" Lisa demanded. "How can I tell if I've been baptized? The teacher said you would know."

Elsa straightened up and faced her daughter. Lisa had grown so much lately that she could almost look the girl in the eye. "No, you're not baptized."

"Why not? Sarah said she was baptized when she was a little baby. Why didn't you have me baptized? Don't you want me to go to heaven?" Lisa followed her mother into the restaurant kitchen. "What about you? Are you baptized? Is dad baptized? How about Jeff and Tony?"

"Stop it!" Elsa snapped at Lisa in a loud whisper. "Everyone will hear you." Already the cook and two waitresses were watching them with interest. "We'll talk about it later, when your father is around."

Business was brisk until nearly three o'clock. Finally Brian and Elsa sat in the back booth to eat their own lunch. They had just started on dessert when Lisa joined them. "Daddy, why haven't I been baptized?" she asked, ignoring her mother. "Sarah's been baptized, and she's going to heaven. I want to go to heaven, too."

"You'll go to heaven, sweetheart," Brian said, eating his chocolate ice cream. "You're a very nice little girl."

Elsa rolled her eyes. She knew what Lisa would say next. "But Sarah's Sunday school teacher says you only get to heaven if you're baptized, daddy."

"Sunday school teachers don't know everything, Lisa," her father said, glancing at Elsa. "We have different ideas in our family."

"Sarah's family goes to church every Sunday, and they go to Sunday school."

Brian finished his ice cream and set the dish aside. "Listen," he said, "a long time ago your mother and I said that we weren't going to influence you kids about any particular church. We said we'd let you decide about religion when you were old enough to understand it all. When you're older, you can figure all that out." Brian smiled at his daughter and started to leave the booth.

"But daddy, I want to decide now," Lisa declared. "I want to be baptized in Sarah's church."

Elsa took a deep breath and blew it out between pursed lips. Brian was frozen in place, staring at his daughter. "Look, sweetheart," Elsa said, gently pushing her daughter. "Why don't you go help at the counter? You can restock the candy shelves. Ask Mike to show you where the boxes are kept, and you can have a candy bar when you're done." Lisa's eyes lit up and she ran to the front of the restaurant.

"Wowee," Brian said, relaxing in the booth. "Just when you're least expecting it, a kid will sock you in the stomach."

"She started talking about it this morning while you were gone," Elsa said. "I stalled her until we could talk it over, but she beat me to it."

"Well, what are we going to do now? Talk about stalling. That's what we've been doing on this religion issue for almost 15 years." Brian chewed on a toothpick. "My mother warned me there'd be a time like this. I never figured it would come when Lisa was 10 years old."

"In our efforts not to influence her, we've left her wide open for anyone's influence, Brian. Now this little friend Sarah and her family have filled her mind with these ideas about Baptism. And we don't even know what kind of church it is." Elsa laughed humorlessly. "You know what? I'd be very happy if all the kids were baptized—finally."

"Oh, stow it away, Elsa. I *know* how you feel after all the arguments we've had about it."

"Well, if we'd settled it when Lisa was a baby, we wouldn't be having this trouble now. Better yet, if we'd settled it before we were married, we could have avoided all the unpleasantness between us and our families. Aunt Becky still won't come to our house."

"No loss there," Brian mumbled. "After I caught her trying to teach Jeff the rosary."

"Yes, you threw her out, and she's never been back." Elsa sighed. "You were so stubborn about it all! Why couldn't we have just joined *my* church? Then the kids would have had a religious upbringing."

"You were the stubborn one. Why couldn't you have joined *my* church? It was nice and simple. The kids would have learned the Bible stories and how to pray properly. But no, you and your family wouldn't hear of it."

"You've never understood, have you, Brian?" Elsa said, glancing around to be sure no one was eavesdropping. "It's better for me just to be fallen away from my church than to join another one."

"Yeah, I remember that song and dance. It's always sounded very selfish to me," Brian said. "Everytime someone suggested that we try this church or that church as a compromise, you started crying and carrying on. By that time Lisa was three years old." He shook his head in disgust. "We were so out of the habit of going to church by then that the argument just died of old age, and we said the kids could decide for themselves later. You know, Elsa, I miss going to church like I did when I was a kid. I really do, and my folks still pray for us."

Elsa's eyes were misty. "My parents say they pray, too. I went to Darlene's wedding a year ago, and the church was so beautiful. I just ached inside. Even now, I wish I could go back."

"You can go. I never stopped you from going to church. Don't lay *that* on me."

"I know you didn't. It was me. I was so embarrassed. But remember that the road runs the other direction, too, Brian. You can go to your church anytime you like." Elsa groped for a tissue in her pocket.

"I haven't been to church in so long I've probably forgotten how to act," he said. "But maybe there's still time after all. Do you suppose?"

"Time for what?" She wiped her eyes with the crumpled tissue she'd resurrected.

"Time to find a church we can agree on. Lisa wants to be baptized. I don't have a problem with that, except now that she's older, I've changed my mind. I do want to have a say about which church she goes to. Jeff and Tony are still small enough to go with us wherever we choose." Brian's expression was hopeful. "What do you say?"

Elsa looked away. "I don't know. What would my family say? How could we ever fit into a different church? The whole thing scares me."

"Are you telling me that after 15 years of marriage, after having three kids, after not going to any church for over 12 years, and now having your daughter wanting to be baptized in some strange church, you're still going to be stubborn? Oh, forget it. This is hopeless!" Brian said, sliding angrily out of the booth. Turning quickly, he bumped into a customer. "Excuse me. Oh, it's you! Elsa, this is the fellow I was telling you about. We had such a good talk the last time he was in to eat. Bob Turner, isn't it?"

"Right. You have a good memory." The man smiled and shook hands with both Brian and Elsa. "I enjoyed our discussion too. I hope I didn't bore you too much with my ideas about our changing society."

"Oh, not at all, Bob. I found it all very interesting, and I learned a lot."

"Brian told me about your talk," Elsa said, sliding out of the booth and standing beside her husband. "We had quite a discussion at home about our own feelings based on what you'd said to Brian."

"Mommy, daddy!" Lisa called, running to them.

"This is our daughter, Lisa," Brian said, putting his arm around her.

"I know it is," Bob said, smiling. "I've met Lisa before."

"Oh, at the candy counter, I'll bet," Elsa said.

"No, mommy," Lisa said. "I met him this morning. This is Pastor Turner, the minister at Sarah's church."

▪ Something to Talk About ▪

1. Describe the situation in Elsa and Brian's home regarding religion. Going back to the time before their marriage, describe the progression of events leading up to Lisa's question about Baptism. How does Elsa feel? How does Brian feel? How has the issue of religion affected their marriage?

2. Why does the religion issue become so crucial in a marriage? Why does the arrival of children complicate the issue and the relationship? How do the couple's parental families enter into the picture? What happens to children when parents do not make the religious decision?

3. Elsa and Brian are both from Christian churches. What if one of the partners had been Jewish? Moslem? Buddhist? an atheist? What pressures would the combination of a Christian and any of the above place upon a marriage relationship?

4. How can a couple either eliminate or dilute the effect of a "mixed religious" marriage before it occurs? Is the only answer to marry someone from your own church? What other suggestions could you make?

5. If you or someone you know well has experienced a marriage with religious differences, tell how the couple coped with the situation. What were the results?

6. How can Christian people outside the marriage reach and/ or witness to a person who has stopped going to church because of religious differences in the marriage? Where do the doors of opportunity seem to be opening in regard to Brian and Elsa's family's spiritual life? What do you think will happen to each person? What difference do you think this will make in the marriage relationship?

20

▪ When Rights and Respect ▪ Are Demanded

"Oh, by the way, Nancy, the awards banquet is on the 17th at the Hilton. I told Mr. Connors we'd both be there," Bruce said, reading the evening paper.

Nancy, printing publicity signs while kneeling on the floor, stopped her work momentarily. "You did what?"

"I told Connors we'd be there." Bruce continued to read the paper.

Nancy looked disgustedly off to one side and pursed her lips. Her toes tapped inside her slippers. "I won't be there, Bruce."

"What?"

"I said, I won't be there."

The newspaper crashed into Bruce's lap. "What do you mean, you won't be there? You *have* to be there. I already said you would be."

"Then you'll just have to say there was a mistake, and I won't be there after all." Nancy spoke carefully and deliberately.

Bruce stared at his wife. "You always go to this banquet with me. It's the company's biggest event of the year. I'm going to get another sales award. You've *got* to go. I'll be embarrassed if you're not there."

Nancy popped the cap on and off her marking pen. "Bruce, I think you owe me the courtesy of inviting me to the banquet before you volunteer me to go. Every year it's the same story with that banquet. I don't have any choice in the matter. And you do it with other things too. Before I know it, you've involved me in the classes at church or the Boy Scout activities or some other deal at your company. I deserve to be asked in advance, and this time I'm not going to go."

"But you're my wife! You go where I go. I have a right to—"

"I have rights, too, Bruce. You want rights and respect? Well, so do I."

The front door slammed. Eric breezed into the middle of the conversation. "I need the car. Let me have the keys, dad." The 16-year-old stood in front of Bruce with his hand out, waiting expectantly.

"You've got to be kidding," Bruce answered angrily. "You can't just sail in here and demand the keys. You've got to show some respect, and you've got to make advance plans with your mother and me. What's the matter with you?"

"Oh, dad, be real! I've got something really important to do with Mike and Craig. We'll just be gone an hour or so. I already told them I could have the car, and they're waiting outside. Come on, be a good guy and give me the keys."

Bruce jumped up and stood in front of his son, nose to nose. The newspaper flew all over Nancy's posters. "Let's get something straight here, Eric. I am your father. You do not order me around. You do what *I* say. Is that clear?"

Eric stood his ground, glaring back. "You have no right to treat me like a little kid. I have my license, I can drive, and you're not using the car right now." Suddenly Eric's voice and demeanor changed. "Please, dad," he begged. "My friends are waiting outside. I'm going to feel like a real flake if I can't have the car. I'm going to be so—"

"Embarrassed?" Nancy asked from the floor.

"Yeah, embarrassed," Eric said. His eyes began to fill with tears.

"Well, I'm sorry," Bruce growled. "You didn't ask me properly or in time. You didn't show any respect for me, and you can't treat me like your slave. No car today, and that's final." He sat down in his chair, his face angry.

Eric looked at his mother in desperation. Nancy shrugged her shoulders. Then Eric swore and ran up the stairs to his room. Heavy footsteps could be heard on the second floor before he raced back down the stairs and out the front door. The whole house shook when the door slammed.

"Can you believe that?" Bruce asked his wife. "Kids today! I never would have spoken to my father like that. I don't understand it. Why does he act like that?"

Nancy didn't say anything. Instead, she pushed the newspapers away and continued printing her signs.

"Well, what's this?" Bruce said angrily. "Don't tell me you condone what that kid just did?"

Nancy clicked her tongue and looked at Bruce with a withering glare. "Are you absolutely deaf and blind? Don't you see what just happened in this room?"

"Yeah! Our son showed gross disrespect."

"No, no. You're missing the whole point," Nancy said, hauling herself to her feet and standing over her husband. She jabbed the marking pen in his direction to emphasize her words. "Think a minute. Just before Eric came in, you said that you'd volunteered me to go to the banquet without asking me first, and you said you'd be embarrassed if I didn't do it. It seemed like a matter of saving face in front of your friends and employer. Then Eric comes in saying that he'd volunteered the car for his friends without asking you first and that he'd be embarrassed if he couldn't have it. That was a matter of saving face in front of *his* friends. Now would you please explain to me what the difference is, Bruce?"

He opened his mouth, but no words came out. Bruce looked puzzled as he gazed first at Nancy and then straight ahead.

"I know you don't like it when I go to my women's rights meetings, Bruce, but I heard something the other day that might help all of us around here." Nancy sat on the sofa. "You just said you don't understand kids today and that you never would have spoken to your father like that."

"Right!" Bruce found his voice. "And I think—"

"Excuse me," Nancy said firmly. "I've got the floor right now. OK, I don't claim to understand them either. But listen to what I heard at my meeting: our whole society is moving from an autocratic, dictatorial attitude to a democratic stance. We see the signs of it all around us. People are demanding the rights they believe are theirs: unions form, minority groups organize, women's organizations develop. It's because people just won't stand for a pyramid type of society anymore. We're talking about equality here."

"All right, wait a minute," Bruce said. "I'm not blind. I see all the changes around me. I don't like them, but I see them. And I'm sorry I volunteered you for that banquet. If you felt like I did when Eric promised his friends the car without asking me first, I can understand that. I assumed too much. I'm *sorry,* but kids can't go around demanding their rights and pushing parents and teachers into corners. Something's wrong with that."

"Of course there is," Nancy replied. "But at least we can begin to see where they get the idea that they have rights. Our whole society is moving in that direction. Actually, Bruce, I think the whole issue rests not on rights, but on respect. And on responsibility."

"Come again?"

"Well, I'm no expert on child raising, but if kids feel even a little bit of what *I* feel, then I can begin to relate to the way they act."

Bruce jerked himself out of the chair and started picking up the scattered newspaper. "I don't want to hear this garbage. You talk as if you lived in a hellhole of some sort. I provide you with a very good living. That's what this banquet is all about. And if you don't want to go—"

"Stop it, Bruce! You always cop out on these conversations, and today you're going to stick it out and hear what I'm saying. You can show me at least that much respect!" With her eyes and rigid expression Nancy dared him to leave.

Bruce hesitated, the rumpled newspaper in his hand. Then he sat down again. "All right, do your worst," he groaned.

Nancy rolled her eyes. "Oh, Bruce, just listen. It won't kill you. Adults and kids alike need to feel worthwhile and as if other people care about them. You don't feel that when the people around you are ordering you about and treating you with disrespect. It seems to me that a person, adult or child, has a right to be spoken to with kindness and to be given some choices. That allows for some responsibility in the relationship. Now tell me the truth, haven't you ever had someone yell at you and make you feel like two cents?"

Bruce looked at his wife and sighed deeply. "Sure I have. It happened yesterday, as a matter of fact. Mr. Connors banged into my office—without even knocking, mind you—and slapped two banquet tickets on my desk. 'Mosley, you've delayed buying these tickets long enough,' he said. 'Come on, pay up. You and your wife have to be at the banquet and that's that.' So I coughed up 50 bucks. He didn't give me any choice. He just ordered me around. I couldn't tell him that money was so scarce this month I really didn't have enough to buy the tickets."

Nancy offered her hand to Bruce. He took it, and they looked at each other for a long moment. "Look," she said.

"Let's calm down about this and talk it over later, OK? We'll work something out. I have an idea that if we just talk to Eric, we can lay down some guidelines with him, too. I love you, Bruce, really I do."

Bruce blinked his eyes rapidly. "I love you, Nancy. More than you'll ever know."

▪ Something to Talk About ▪

1. Describe the situation in this home. How is Bruce feeling? What system of behavior and response does he use? What are Nancy's feelings? What system is she trying to use? What about Eric? How does his attitude reflect that which he experiences in his home?

2. Examine Nancy's words: "Our whole society is moving from an autocratic, dictatorial attitude to a democratic stance." What evidences do you see in society that show this to be true? How does this move affect marriages? How does it affect children growing up during the shift?

3. Everyone wants to be respected. What does it mean to respect your husband? to respect your wife? to respect your child? to respect your parents? Give examples of situations in which respect is or isn't shown. Does respect mean fear or love? How is respect fostered in a relationship?

4. Rights involve responsibilities. What responsibilities does Bruce have toward Nancy? does Nancy have toward Bruce? How does this carry over into parent-child relationships?

5. Nancy and Bruce affirm their love for each other even in the face of their differences. Read 1 Corinthians 13. Note especially the verses that describe relationships. Apply these to a marriage in the light of rights, respect, and responsibilities.

▪ Research Questionnaire ▪

This questionnaire was completed by many couples as part of the research program for this book. Individuals and couples may find the open-ended statements to be valuable in self-understanding and in opening communication in their relationships. Small groups may also find value in sharing responses to the open-ended statements.

1. To me, marriage should be . . .
2. Communication in marriage is . . .
3. Having children affects a marriage by . . .
4. When in-laws live near a married couple, . . .
5. I think the housework should be . . .
6. The biggest problem married couples face is . . .
7. When one partner in a marriage is a Christian and the other isn't, . . .
8. In a marriage in which one partner is addicted to alcohol or drugs, . . .
9. When a great tragedy strikes a family, the married couple . . .
10. The biggest problem facing retired couples is . . .
11. When the wife has a career as well as the husband, . . .

12. The best way to foster communication in marriage is . . .
13. If a couple does not have children, . . .
14. When the partners in marriage belong to different churches, . . .
15. A couple who has previously been married to others will . . .
16. When a parent or parent-in-law lives with a married couple, . . .
17. When the breadwinner in a family is unemployed, . . .
18. If the partners in a marriage have "fallen out of love," . . .
19. The role of the church in a marriage . . .
20. When adult children live with a married couple, . . .
21. Whenever I hear that a friend of mine is getting divorced, I think . . .
22. When a woman earns more money than her husband, . . .
23. When one partner has been unfaithful to the other, . . .
24. I think physical abuse in a marriage . . .
25. When a couple moves to a new location, . . .
26. The role of in-laws in a marriage . . .
27. When a married couple is having problems, they should . . .
28. If the breadwinner spends all his or her time working and rarely sees the spouse or family, . . .
29. When one marriage partner is dominant over the other, . . .
30. A person who is being physically abused in a marriage relationship should . . .
31. When marriage partners constantly criticize each other, . . .
32. If I could give a newlywed some advice about marriage, I'd say . . .